Rapid Application Development with AWS Amplify

Build cloud-native mobile and web apps from scratch through continuous delivery and test automation

Adrian Leung

BIRMINGHAM—MUMBAI

Rapid Application Development with AWS Amplify

Copyright © 2021 Packt Publishing

Associate Group Product Manager: Pavan Ramchandani
Publishing Product Manager: Rohit Rajkumar
Senior Editor: Sofi Rogers
Content Development Editor: Rakhi Patel
Technical Editor: Shubham Sharma
Copy Editor: Safis Editing
Project Coordinator: Manthan Patel
Proofreader: Safis Editing
Indexer: Manju Arasan
Production Designer: Roshan Kawale

First published: June 2021
Production reference: 1250621

Published by Packt Publishing Ltd.
Livery Place
35 Livery Street
Birmingham
B3 2PB, UK.

ISBN 978-1-80020-723-3

www.packt.com

Contributors

About the author

Adrian Leung is a full-stack cloud native engineer and Agile Transformation Coach with a deep understanding of Business and Organizational Agilities. His background has led him to coach many enterprises in digital transformation with Design Thinking and Agile as well as enterprise scalable cloud-native solution architectures to deliver real value to their customers.

Adrian earned a degree in Applied Information Technology from The University of Newcastle, Australia in 2007. His work history includes helping many enterprises in Hong Kong with their digital transformation journey. He is currently the Founder of Adventvr that is building amazing products and espousing the benefits of serverless systems whenever he has the chance.

I want to thank the people who have been close to me and supported me from all over the world.

About the reviewer

Grégoire Hertault is a full-stack web developer based in France. With over 10 years of experience, he has become an expert in a wide range of technologies, including React, React Native, and AWS. He is the author of React Admin Amplify, an open source library designed to easily set up the admin interface of your AWS Amplify app. He is also the author of React Native Twilio Phone, a VoIP module for React Native. Besides open source projects, he works as a technical expert for start-ups and large companies.

Table of Contents

Section 2: Building a Photo Sharing App

3

Pluggable Amplify UI Components

4

User Management with Amplify Authentication

5

Creating a Blog Post with Amplify GraphQL

Section 3: Production Readiness

9

Setting Up a Custom Domain Name and the Amplify Admin UI

Other Books You May Enjoy

Index

Preface

The worldwide market of public cloud infrastructure is worth roughly around 100 billion US dollars. Do you know who the leading cloud provider is in 2020? AWS is the leading cloud provider, and is powering 33% of the world's cloud infrastructure, which is more than Microsoft Azure and Google Cloud Platform combined. Therefore, it's a no-brainer to choose AWS over other cloud providers for your next project. But you might think moving from traditional bare-metal or virtual machine infrastructure might be a huge learning curve for you, or you might think you will need to invest a lot of money to train up your development team to adopt new technologies. AWS Amplify is coming to the rescue. AWS Amplify is a set of robust toolchains that can bootstrap full-stack cloud-native web and mobile application development. It abstracts the complexity away from setting up the AWS cloud ecosystem, which empowers your development team to build products much quicker than ever before.

AWS Amplify comes with helpful resources, such as ready-to-use UI components, machine learning capabilities, and a user management system, plus enterprise-grade security, scalability, and high availability, which gives you peace of mind in the modern tech world. This book is dedicated to helping you and your team to become very hands-on with AWS Amplify and being able to build modern full stack cloud-native apps with ease. Most well-known companies use AWS technologies without you knowing. You can check out their case studies at the following link:

```
https://aws.amazon.com/solutions/case-studies/
```

Prior to starting writing this book, my own business has delivered an enterprise product with AWS Amplify for our client in less than 3 months. So, I realized how AWS Amplify could empower and benefit development teams with its powerful toolchains. The most amazing part is the DevOps pipeline with test automation capabilities, which enable the development team to start shipping the product to the customer's hands in minutes, tested thoroughly by machines automatically instead of waiting for weeks of manual testing. AWS has done an absolutely phenomenal job with Serverless and NoOps (otherwise known as LessOps). You can now implement the latest cloud-native architectures with AWS Amplify easily. Moving your legacy system to the cloud is easier than ever before. Therefore, both production and development teams can spend more time developing new features for the customers instead of fiddling around with DevOps or DevSecOps practices, such as Continuous Deployment, Security, Manual User Acceptance Tests, and deployment. Back in the old days, DevSecOps required a massive team and weeks of preparation for each deployment, and now it's all about scripting with a small team or even a one-man band. If your company has adopted Agile and DevOps in the past or has started looking into adopting Agile and DevOps, you could get a head start with AWS Amplify.

How long do you think you will need to build your next app and publish it as a website or to an app store with AWS Amplify? Months? Weeks? Well, let's find out by going through each chapter of this book. Find a quiet spot and let's get started.

Who this book is for

This book is for developers and tech companies looking to develop cloud-native products rapidly with the AWS ecosystem, especially those who want to adopt cloud-native practices as part of their digital transformation strategy. Web and mobile developers with little to no experience of TypeScript programming will also find this book helpful. Although no prior experience with AWS or TypeScript is required, basic familiarity with modern frameworks such as React and React Native is useful.

What this book covers

Chapter 1, *Getting Familiar with the Amplify CLI and Amplify Console,* familiarizes you with the Amplify CLI and Amplify Console so you can decide how to set up and configure a new or existing project with AWS Amplify. You will learn how to integrate Amplify with existing projects with the most popular frameworks.

Chapter 2, *Creating a React App with AmplifyJS and TypeScript*, explains how to create and launch an app with React with TypeScript within no time. You will also create a React app at the same time with some small adjustments.

Chapter 3, Pluggable Amplify UI components, covers how to add pre-built Amplify UI Components to your app, such as a user signup form or a photo picker.

Chapter 4, User Management with Amplify Authentication, explains how to add user management to your app with Amplify Authentication and Amplify UI Components.

Chapter 5, Creating a Blog Post with Amplify GraphQL, covers advanced GraphQL techniques to insert and query data between users and DynamoDB with queries, mutations, and subscriptions.

Chapter 6, Uploading and Sharing Photos with Amplify Storage, explains how to add the photo upload feature to the app with the ready-made React Photo Picker UI component and AWS Amplify Storage, as well as how to list images with a photo album.

Chapter 7, Setting Up an Amplify Pipeline, covers the setup of the DevOps pipeline with Amplify, including adding the YAML config file to the repository, troubleshooting techniques, and different ways to trigger the pipeline.

Chapter 8, Test Automation with Cypress, explains how to set up your project with Cypress and Cucumber, how to write executable User Stories in Gherkin, and how to write test cases as Step Definitions with TypeScript.

Chapter 9, Setting Up a Custom Domain Name and the Amplify Admin UI, shows you how to set up a custom domain name with your Amplify project on the Amplify Console with Route 53 so that you can tell the world about the new photo-sharing app that you have just created.

To get the most out of this book

In order to get most out of this book, you should install the integrated development environment (IDE) that is available with the operating system that you are using:

IDE Software covered in the book	OS Requirements
VSCode 1.57.0+ (IDE)	Windows, macOS, and Linux (any distribution)
Android Studio 4.2.1+ (IDE)	Windows, macOS, and Linux (any distribution)
Xcode 12.4+ (IDE)	macOS only (optional)

Libraries covered in the book	OS Requirements
React 17+	Windows, macOS, and Linux (any distribution)
React Native 0.64+	Windows, macOS, and Linux (any distribution)
Expo SDK 41+	Windows, macOS, and Linux (any distribution)
TypeScript 4.3.2+	Windows, macOS, and Linux (any distribution)

If you are using the digital version of this book, we advise you to type the code yourself or access the code via the GitHub repository (link available in the next section). Doing so will help you avoid any potential errors related to the copying and pasting of code.

Download the example code files

You can download the example code files for this book from your account at `www.packt.com`. If you purchased this book elsewhere, you can visit `www.packtpub.com/support` and register to have the files emailed directly to you.

You can download the code files by following these steps:

1. Log in or register at `www.packt.com`.
2. Select the **Support** tab.
3. Click on **Code Downloads**.
4. Enter the name of the book in the **Search** box and follow the onscreen instructions.

Once the file is downloaded, please make sure that you unzip or extract the folder using the latest version of:

- 7-Zip for Windows
- Archive Utility for macOS
- 7-Zip for Linux

The code bundle for the book is also hosted on GitHub at `https://github.com/PacktPublishing/Rapid-Application-Development-with-AWS-Amplify`. In case there's an update to the code, it will be updated on the existing GitHub repository.

We also have other code bundles from our rich catalog of books and videos available at `https://github.com/PacktPublishing/`. Check them out!

Download the color images

We also provide a PDF file that has color images of the screenshots/diagrams used in this book. You can download it here: `https://static.packt-cdn.com/downloads/9781800207233_ColorImages.pdf`.

Conventions used

There are a number of text conventions used throughout this book.

`Code in text`: Indicates code words in text, database table names, folder names, filenames, file extensions, pathnames, dummy URLs, user input, and Twitter handles. Here is an example: "The next step is to go to the specific project directory and call the `amplify add auth` command in the terminal in order to set up the Amplify UI Authenticator."

A block of code is set as follows:

```
    sectionFooterLink: {
        fontSize: 16,
        color: buttonColor,
        alignItems: 'baseline',
        textAlign: 'center',
    },
    sectionFooterLinkDisabled: {
        fontSize: 16,
        color: disabledButtonColor,
        alignItems: 'baseline',
        textAlign: 'center',
    },
```

Any command-line input or output is written as follows:

```
yarn add aws-amplify @aws-amplify/ui-react
```

Bold: Indicates a new term, an important word, or words that you see onscreen. For example, words in menus or dialog boxes appear in the text like this. Here is an example: "Now click the **Run on Android emulator** button on the browser to check out the Expo app on Android."

> **Tips or important notes**
> Appear like this.

Share Your Thoughts

Once you've read *Rapid Application Development with AWS Amplify*, we'd love to hear your thoughts! Scan the QR code below to go straight to the Amazon review page for this book and share your feedback.

https://packt.link/r/1800207239

Your review is important to us and the tech community and will help us make sure we're delivering excellent quality content.

Section 1: Getting Ready

In this section, you will learn how to set up a project with the latest and most popular frameworks, such as React, Ionic Angular, and Vue, as well as learn how to deploy a project to a staging environment with an AWS Amplify DevOps pipeline for CI/CD.

In this section, there are the following chapters:

- *Chapter 1, Getting Familiar with the Amplify CLI and Amplify Console*
- *Chapter 2, Creating a React App with AmplifyJS and TypeScript*

1
Getting Familiar with the Amplify CLI and Amplify Console

In order to understand what **Amazon Web Services Amplify** (**AWS Amplify**) is and how to use it to create an app successfully, we will need to understand the fundamentals of the AWS Amplify ecosystem and how it connects to each of its own components, such as the AWS Amplify **command-line interface** (**CLI**) and the **AWS Amplify Console** (**Amplify Console**), to maximize the benefit of using it.

The AWS Amplify CLI is a toolchain that provides a robust set of features to simplify cloud-native mobile development. AWS Amplify is framework-agnostic itself because it supports all the major frameworks out there, such as React, React Native, Angular, Ionic, Vue, and pure JavaScript. Therefore, any team can easily pick it up immediately to integrate it with their existing project or create a new project with AWS Amplify. Since React is one of the most popular frameworks at the moment and TypeScript has become a common language for full-stack developments, we will be using these frameworks to create examples throughout this book.

Amplify Console is not just a cloud admin console—it also allows developers to easily deploy and host their cloud-native full-stack serverless apps. It supports a Git-based workflow, **continuous deployment (CD)** of the serverless backend and frontend with the DevOps pipeline, end-to-end test automation, globally available web hosting with a **content delivery network (CDN)**, and more. All of these features are only a few clicks away with the easy-to-configure console interface. Amplify Console accelerates the development cycle by streamlining the **continuous integration (CI)** and CD workflow and abstracts away the complexity of setting up a fully working DevOps pipeline, which enables your development team to focus on development without wasting time fiddling around with infrastructure and pipelines. It empowers your development team with a state-of-the-art workflow and pipeline, helping them to deliver products much more quickly with better quality than ever before.

In this chapter, we're going to learn how to start an AWS Amplify project by familiarizing ourselves with the toolchain, runtime, AWS Amplify CLI, and Amplify Console on the AWS cloud. We will go through each of these in order to be able to set up and configure a new or existing project with AWS Amplify after having read this chapter. We will learn about the possibilities of integrating Amplify with existing projects, working with the most popular frameworks.

We're going to cover the following main topics:

- Understanding the AWS Amplify CLI
- Exploring Amplify Console
- Understanding AWS Amplify hosting
- Creating full-stack serverless web and native apps with AWS Amplify

Technical requirements

Development of Amplify and React apps can be done in all major **operating systems** (**OSes**), such as Windows, macOS, and Linux, so you don't need to worry about which OS you should choose. The best OS is the one that you are most familiar with. Therefore, our commands and scripts will be focused on something that could be run across all platforms. First things first—you will need to install a code editor, a JavaScript runtime, and a package manager before you can start to develop React apps. These are the technologies and installations required for creating an AWS Amplify app with React and TypeScript:

- Install an open source cross-platform code editor. We would recommend using **Visual Studio Code** (**VS Code**) because VS Code and TypeScript are created by Microsoft, so TypeScript support is out of the box. For more information, visit `https://code.visualstudio.com/`.

- Alternatively, you could choose Atom, which is another very popular open source and cross-platform code editor out there, but you will need to install the TypeScript plugin yourself after installation. For more information, visit `https://atom.io/`.

- In order to download the TypeScript plugin for Atom, you can click the **Install** button on the following web page after you have installed the Atom editor:

  `https://atom.io/packages/atom-typescript`

- Install the open source cross-platform Node.js JavaScript runtime environment:

- Since Linux, Windows with **Windows Subsystem for Linux** (**WSL 2**), and macOS all support Homebrew, we will use Homebrew to install all of our dependencies. For more information, visit `https://brew.sh/`.

- Once you have installed Homebrew, you can use the following command to install Node.js:

```
brew install node
```

- Install an open source and cross-platform package manager for development. We could install it with an installer from the following link:

  `https://classic.yarnpkg.com/en/docs/install`

- Alternatively, we could use Homebrew to install Yarn by running the following command:

```
brew install yarn
```

Once you have completed all the preceding installation steps, you will then be ready to start developing AWS Amplify apps. Prior experience with TypeScript and React is not required, but you could go through a few tutorials by yourself if you are interested in studying the fundamentals of TypeScript and React. Further details are provided here:

- TypeScript documentation: `https://www.typescriptlang.org/docs/home.html`

- Hello World tutorial for TypeScript: `https://code.visualstudio.com/docs/typescript/typescript-tutorial`

- Tutorial and documentation for React: `https://reactjs.org/`

All the code and instructions in this book can be found at the following **Uniform Resource Locator (URL)**:

```
https://github.com/PacktPublishing/Rapid-Application-
Development-with-AWS-Amplify/tree/master/ch1
```

> **Important note**
>
> We will be using both the npm and Yarn package managers to install dependencies, but npm already comes with Node.js, so there is no need to install it separately. The reason behind this is some of the tools such as the Amplify CLI would have issues on Linux if we were to use Yarn but would not have issues with npm, for some reason, so we will use what works across all OSes in this book.

Understanding the AWS Amplify CLI

Before we get started on the Amplify CLI, we might need to create an account on AWS first. To do so, go to `https://aws.amazon.com/`.

Please note that AWS comes with a Free Tier for beginners, therefore creating your Amplify app for development on AWS should be free at the beginning, as long as our usage is within the Free Tier. Once we have created an AWS account, we can go ahead and install the AWS Amplify CLI with the following command:

```
yarn global add @aws-amplify/cli
```

The preceding command will install the CLI globally. The AWS Amplify CLI is a toolchain that aims to simplify your workflow with the AWS ecosystem. You may wonder what is under the hood of the AWS Amplify CLI. Basically, it connects with the AWS ecosystem through the CLI. Every modern app requires features such as authentication, **machine learning** (**ML**), a NoSQL database, object storage, analytics, web hosting, a serverless **application programming interface** (**API**) gateway, notifications, and so on. AWS Amplify comes with them all. Everything you need to do is just a few commands away.

Here are a few of the most commonly used commands for us to use during development:

Command	Description
`amplify configure`	Configure project settings.
`amplify init`	Initialize a new project.
`amplify configure project`	Reconfigure project settings.

`amplify add <category>`	Add a cloud feature to the project, such as authentication and an API, as follows:
	
	Hosting:
	
	`amplify add hosting`
	
	Authentication:
	
	`amplify add auth`
	
	Simple Storage Service (**S3**) and DynamoDB storage:
	
	`amplify add storage`
	
	GraphQL or a RESTful API (REST stands for REpresentational State Transfer):
	
	`amplify add api`

`amplify update <category>`	Update a cloud feature (check out the next table for more details about different categories).
`amplify push`	Provision cloud resources with the local code. If you want to override your local AppSync resolvers and templates, you could add a flag such as this: `amplify push --no-gql-override`
`amplify pull`	Fetch the changes from the cloud
`amplify codegen add`	Generate code that is based on the GraphQL schema.
`amplify help`	Display help information for the CLI.

The previous table shows the commands of the AWS Amplify CLI and the mentioned categories. The following table outlines each category with its matching AWS products:

Category	AWS Product
Auth	Amazon Cognito
Storage	Amazon S3 and Amazon DynamoDB
Function	AWS Lambda
API	AWS AppSync and Amazon API Gateway
Analytics	Amazon Pinpoint
Hosting	Amazon S3 and Amazon CloudFront
Notifications	Amazon Pinpoint
Interactions	Amazon Lex
Predictions	Amazon Rekognition, Amazon Textract, Amazon Translate, Amazon Polly, Amazon Transcribe, Amazon Comprehend, and Amazon SageMaker

As you can see, with its cloud offerings, AWS Amplify simplifies the integration for you by abstracting away the complex setup and wiring between your app and each AWS product—such as generating necessary code behind the scenes—through the Amplify CLI.

If you have an existing project with supported frameworks (such as React, React Native, Angular, Ionic, Vue, or even native iOS and Android apps) that you would like to integrate with AWS Amplify, you could simply call `amplify configure` and `amplify init` at any time to set up the project. If you want to initialize a new project with Amplify after the project creation with the supported framework of your choice, all you need to do is call the same commands too. By calling those initiation commands through the Amplify CLI in the terminal, it will connect directly to Amplify Console through the terminal and the web browser under the hood, which will create and configure resources for the developer. Imagine the Amplify CLI as a setup wizard and Amplify Console as the **user interface (UI)** to create and configure an Amplify project.

We have just learned the basics of the Amplify CLI by following the steps of how to set it up. You might still need to have a better understanding of what you can do with it and how it can power up your next project. We will show you how to connect seamlessly to Amplify Console from the AWS Amplify CLI with a few simple commands next.

> **Important note**
>
> If you want to follow the latest changes to the Amplify CLI or report a bug that you have encountered, add the AWS Amplify CLI repository to your Favorites with the following link:
>
> https://github.com/aws-amplify/amplify-cli/

Exploring Amplify Console

In this section, we will go through Amplify Console in order to learn how to set up an Amplify project properly. Let's enter the `amplify configure` command in the terminal, as illustrated in the following code snippet, and this will open up the default browser of your machine and take you to the **AWS Management Console**:

```
amplify configure
```

1. Once you have entered the preceding command, it will open up the browser and ask you to log in to your AWS account, as shown in the following snippet. After you have logged in to your AWS account, return back to the terminal and hit *Enter* to continue:

    ```
    Follow these steps to set up access to your AWS account:
    Sign in to your AWS administrator account:
    https://console.aws.amazon.com/
    Press Enter to continue
    ```

2. It will then ask you to select your AWS region by using the up- and down-arrow keys and then hitting *Enter* to select a region, as follows:

    ```
    Specify the AWS Region? region: (Use arrow keys)
    ❯ us-east-1
      us-east-2
      us-west-2
      eu-west-1
      eu-west-2
      eu-central-1
      ap-northeast-1
    (Move up and down to reveal more choices)
    ```

3. Type your desired AWS **Identity and Access Management (IAM)** username or hit
    Enter with the suggested username, as shown in the following snippet. The prefix
    with the `amplify` username will help you identify and remember the specific IAM
    user on the IAM Management Console, so call it something that's relevant to your
    project name, such as `amplify-project-name`:

    ```
    Specify the AWS Region
    ? region:  us-east-1
    Specify the username of the new IAM user:
    ? user name: (amplify-XXXXX)
    ```

4. It will open up the browser and take you to the **IAM Management Console**. The
    username is pre-filled for you, and it also selects the correct access type for you,
    which is programmatic access. Programmatic access options allow the CLI to save
    an encrypted access key ID and an access secret key locally on your development
    machine. This allows the CLI to have access rights to configure the project for you
    without entering a password every time. So, leave it as is and hit **Next: Permissions**
    to continue, as illustrated in the following screenshot:

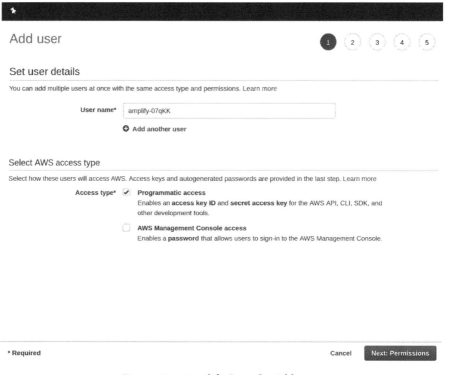

Figure 1.1 – Amplify Console: Add user

5. In order to allow the Amplify CLI and your project to have access to all features of AWS, you should set the policies by attaching the `AdministratorAccess` policy. You could customize your own policy for a specific project as well. By default, it has selected the right policy for you, so click **Next: Tags** to continue, as illustrated in the following screenshot:

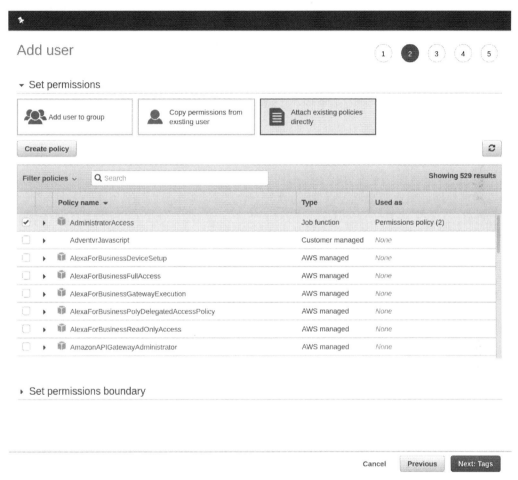

Figure 1.2 – Amplify Console: Set permissions

6. On the **Add tags** screen, please add some useful custom key-value pair tags for you to identify and remember who has access to this IAM user. You could add a specific developer's name as the key and an email address as the value, or a name of a project as the key and `amplify` as the value, in order to remember that this IAM user is created for your specific Amplify project. You can always come back to the IAM console through the AWS console to add or remove IAM users or edit its access policies if you make any mistakes throughout this process. After you have created several tags, you can click **Next: Review** to continue, as illustrated in the following screenshot:

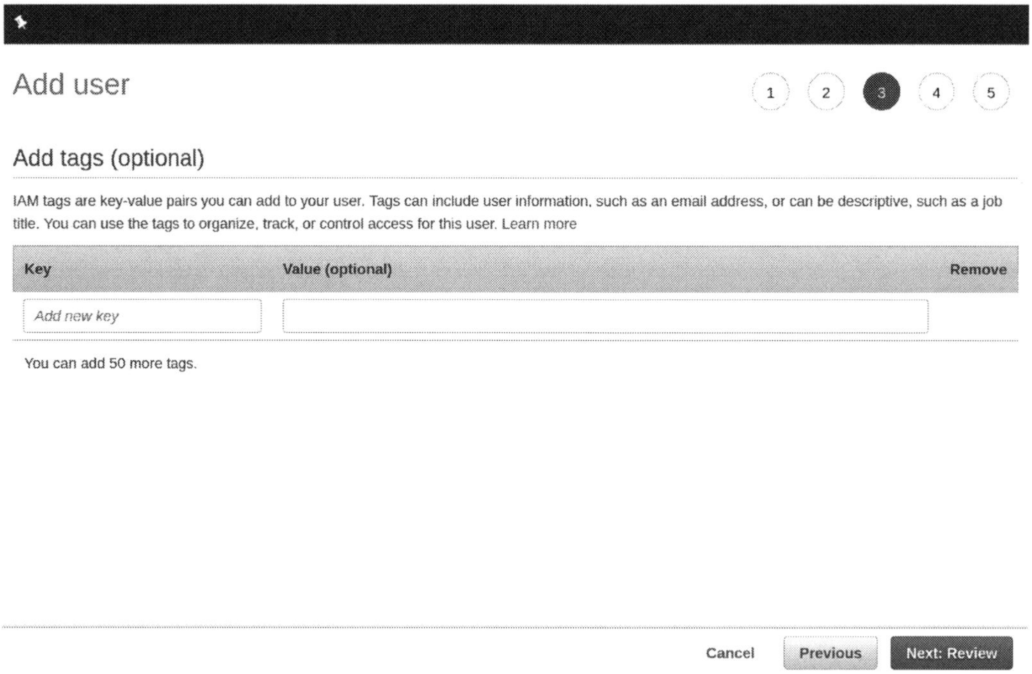

Add user   ① ② ⬤ ④ ⑤

Add tags (optional)

IAM tags are key-value pairs you can add to your user. Tags can include user information, such as an email address, or can be descriptive, such as a job title. You can use the tags to organize, track, or control access for this user. Learn more

Key	Value (optional)	Remove
Add new key		

You can add 50 more tags.

Cancel   Previous   Next: Review

Figure 1.3 – Amplify Console: Add tags

7. On the **Review** screen, you can double-check every detail before creating an IAM user. If you made any mistakes during the previous steps, you can click **Previous** to go back to the previous steps to make changes. You can simply click **Create User** and it will create a new IAM user for you, as well as generating an access key and a secret key, as illustrated in the following screenshot:

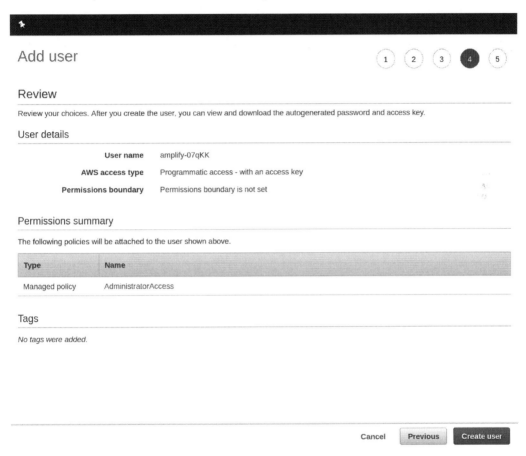

Figure 1.4 – Amplify Console: Review and Create user

8. As you can see, the IAM Management Console has created an IAM user for you
    and has generated an access key and a secret key. You can download a `.csv` file
    that contains the access key ID and the secret key as a backup first by clicking the
    Download .csv button, as illustrated in the following screenshot. Then, you can
    copy and paste both the access key ID and secret key from here and return back
    to the terminal for the next step. Leave the browser open and return back to the
    terminal:

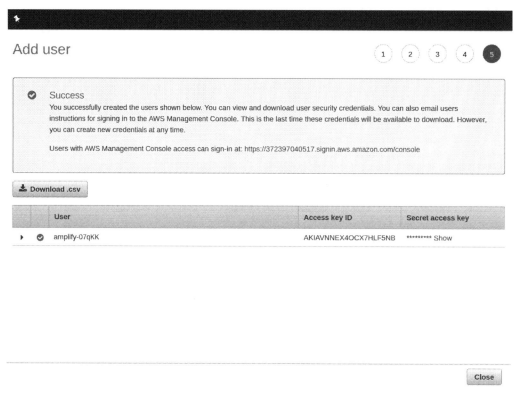

Figure 1.5 – Amplify Console: Downloading user credentials

9. Once you have completed the user creation process and returned back to the
    terminal, you will see the following message. Hit *Enter* to continue:

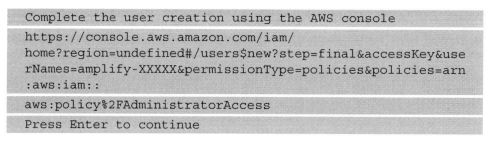

10. The CLI will ask you to enter the access key ID and the secret access key. You could go back to the browser or open the `.csv` file to copy and paste them in the terminal, as follows:

```
Enter the access key of the newly created user:
? accessKeyId:   (<YOUR_ACCESS_KEY_ID>)
? secretAccessKey:   (<YOUR_SECRET_ACCESS_KEY>)
```

11. The Amplify CLI will ask you to either update or create an AWS profile on your local machine. If you have set the IAM user with the default admin access rights, it makes sense to use it across all projects. You can simply hit *Enter* to continue with the suggested name, `default`, as illustrated in the following snippet; otherwise, type your desired memorable profile name that is related to the IAM user and hit *Enter* to continue:

```
This would update/create the AWS Profile in your local
machine
? Profile Name:   (default)
```

12. Amplify Console will let you know once the new user has been set up successfully by showing a message like this:

```
This would update/create the AWS Profile in your local
machine
? Profile Name:   default

Successfully set up the new user.
```

> **Important note**
> If you want to learn more about how AWS Amplify CLI and Amplify Console work, you can visit the Amplify Console website at the following link:
> `https://console.aws.amazon.com/amplify/home`

Now that you have become familiar with the AWS Amplify CLI and Amplify Console in this section, we will discover AWS Amplify hosting in the next section.

Understanding AWS Amplify hosting

Amplify hosting is a part of the Amplify Console toolchain that helps you to host the static artifact of a web app on AWS S3 with the AWS CloudFront CDN. All you need to do is to call `amplify add hosting` to add the capability to the app. After you have created an AWS profile through the CLI and console, you can set up AWS Amplify hosting with your repository, as follows:

1. Click on the `https://console.aws.amazon.com/amplify/home` link and then click on the hamburger menu (triple lines) at the top-left corner to see the options, as illustrated in the following screenshot:

Figure 1.6 – Amplify Console: Home page

2. Click **All apps** on the menu, then click **Connect app**, as illustrated in the following screenshot:

Figure 1.7 – Amplify Console: All apps

3. In this step, you have the following three options:

- We are going to choose the **From your existing code** option, so you can either clone the project of this book or create a new project on your preferred Git repository and click **Continue**.

- Since the samples for the **From fullstack samples** option are written in JavaScript and not in TypeScript, we won't go through them in this book.

- If you select **From scratch**, it will then take you to the AWS Amplify documentation website at `https://aws-amplify.github.io/docs/`.

The aforementioned options can be seen in the following screenshot:

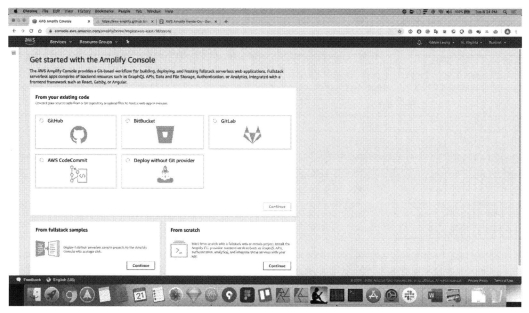

Figure 1.8 – Amplify Console: Git repository

4. Now, you will need to create a new project using one of the following Git repository providers that are supported by AWS Amplify:

- GitHub

- Bitbucket (`https://support.atlassian.com/bitbucket-cloud/docs/create-a-git-repository/`)

- GitLab

- AWS CodeCommit

- Deploy without Git provider (upload a ZIP file that contains the artifacts manually)

    Bitbucket provides unlimited free repositories for organization and personal accounts, which is ideal for beginners. Jira has become the de facto choice for enterprises and software companies to manage their software delivery in the last 10 years. Both Bitbucket and Jira are developed by Atlassian, so if you are planning to use or are already using Jira, then it makes sense to use Bitbucket for your repositories because the integration between the two is seamless.

5. Let's choose Bitbucket and click **Continue**, and connect to the repository that you have created on Bitbucket.

Let's say you have created new Amplify projects in a repository; in that case, you can always come back here to connect your new app through Amplify Console. Now that you are familiar with AWS Amplify hosting, we will create some full-stack serverless web and native apps with AWS Amplify in the next section.

Creating full-stack serverless web and native apps with AWS Amplify

In order to connect AWS Console with a Git repository provider, we will need to create our Git repository first. Let's assume you have created a new blank project in one of the Git repositories we mentioned earlier. Open the terminal and choose your path, as outlined next, to create your first AWS Amplify app with either React, React Native, or React Native with Expo. I have put together the following table for you to decide which options to choose from, and they can be all written in TypeScript:

Option	Pros and Cons	Command

Expo	Pros:
	
	1. One code base for iOS, Android, and web.
	
	2. Online build services for iOS and Android, which is ideal for those who do not own a Mac with a managed workflow (I will explain the different workflows in the next step).
	
	3. Same performance as React Native.
	
	Cons:
	
	1. Developing with native code requires a bare workflow and the cloud build service is not yet ready for that, which means that if you do not own a Mac and are not planning to buy one, you will need to wait for the Expo team to finish the development for the cloud build service for the bare workflow.
	
	2. Navigation and components might not be able to share between web and native platforms. You might need to write additional code to detect and use different components for different platforms.
		`yarn global add expo-cli`
		
		`expo init my-app`
		
		`choose expo-template-blank-typescript`

Option	Pros and Cons	Command
React	Pros: Build web app. Cons: You will need to create a separate code base for iOS and Android apps.	`npx create-react-app my-app --template typescript`
React Native	Pros: 1. Build native iOS and Android app. 2. Build native app for Windows (including PC and Xbox) and macOS (`https://aka.ms/ReactNative`). Cons: 1. You will need to create a separate code base for your web app. 2. A Mac is required to develop an iOS app.	`npx react-native init MyApp --template react-native-template-typescript`

Creating an Expo app

I personally consider Expo the go-to option for most new projects, especially for **proofs of concept (POCs)**, because it supports both mobile devices (iOS and Android) and web devices but at the same time gives you the native performance of React Native. If later in your project you need to write custom native scripts for iOS and Android platforms, then you have two options—either eject the Expo app altogether with the `expo eject` command or select a new bare workflow from the start.

There are two workflows that you can choose from when you are developing a React Native app with Expo: a managed workflow and a bare workflow. With a managed workflow, you only write JavaScript/TypeScript, and Expo tools and services take care of everything else for you. With a bare workflow, you have full control over every aspect of a native project, but Expo tools and services are a little more limited. I have put together the following table for you to decide which workflow to choose:

Feature	Managed Workflow	Bare Workflow
Develop apps with only JavaScript/TypeScript	☑	
Use Expo build service to create your iOS and Android builds	☑	In progress but not yet available
Use Expo's push notification service	☑	☑
Use Expo's over-the-air updates features	☑	☑
Develop with the Expo client app	☑	☑
Access to the Expo software development kit (SDK)	☑	☑
Add custom native code and manage native dependencies		☑
Develop in Xcode and Android Studio		☑

Let's go ahead and create a React Native app with Expo by entering a few commands in the terminal:

1. Run the following command in the terminal in order to create a React Expo app:

```
expo init my-app
```

2. Since we want to write our code once and run it on iOS, Android, and the web with TypeScript, we will choose blank (TypeScript) in the terminal, as follows:

```
? Choose a template:
    ----- Managed workflow -----
    Blank: a minimal app as clean as an empty canvas
  > blank (TypeScript) same as blank but with TypeScript
    configuration
    Tabs: several example screens and tabs using react-
    navigation
    ----- Bare workflow -----
    minimal bare and minimal, just the essentials to get
    you started
```

```
minimal (TypeScript) same as minimal but with
TypeScript
configuration
```

3. Once it's done, you can use the following commands to start running and developing the Expo app:

Command	Description
yarn start	This will open the Metro bundler in the browser and let you select how to run the app.
yarn ios	This will open the Metro bundler in the browser, and then open the iOS simulator and download and run the Expo client app with the iOS app, which might take a while.
yarn android	This will open the Metro bundler in the browser, and then open the Android emulator and download and run the Expo client app with the Android app, which might take a while.
yarn web	This will open the Metro bundler in the browser, and then open the web app on the browser shortly after.
Ctrl + C	To close the server and bundler altogether.

Alternatively, you can run the create-react-native-app command, as shown in the following code snippet, to create an Expo app. This has done all the hardwiring for you, such as configuration with iOS and Android projects:

```
npx create-react-native-app -t with-typescript
```

For iOS apps only, you will need one extra step, which requires a macOS computer. Change the directory to the ios folder under the project folder and run this command in order to install the CocoaPods dependencies:

```
cd ios && pod install
```

As you might have realized, the create-react-native-app command supports both web and native apps. You could actually focus on this path to create both React web and native apps instead of creating two projects. You can learn more about the differences between Expo and React Native at this link: https://reactnative.dev/docs/environment-setup.

Let's create an app with Expo first so that we can actually experience what Expo is like compared to pure React Native afterward, with firsthand experience. If you are not targeting iOS, you can skip the iOS exercise; the same goes for Android and the web. Feel free to jump to the one you're most interested in starting with.

Developing for iOS

If your Mac did not have Xcode installed, please go to the Mac App Store to download the Xcode app first. You can install Xcode from the Mac App Store with this link: `https://apps.apple.com/us/app/xcode/id497799835?mt=12`. You will then be taken to the following page:

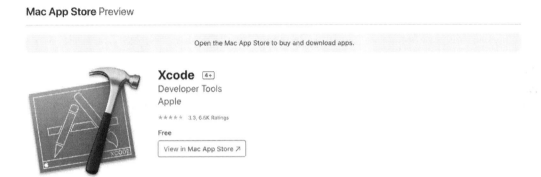

Figure 1.9 – Xcode

Once you have installed Xcode on your Mac, go to the terminal and enter the following command in order to build and launch the Expo iOS app:

```
yarn ios
```

You will see the following screen as the app is built, installed, and launched on the iOS simulator (which is part of Xcode):

Figure 1.10 – iPhone simulator

Since the screen is asking you to open up the App.tsx file on your project to start working on your app, go to the code editor and edit the App.tsx file, change the text on the screen to something that you like, and save it (*Command + S* on a Mac or *Ctrl + S* on a PC/Linux). You should then be able to see that the app has changed accordingly in real time on the iOS simulator, and that's how we can confirm that the setup and workflow is working, as illustrated in the following screenshot:

Figure 1.11 – iPhone simulator with the Expo CLI

You should now have a good understanding of how Expo works with iOS. We will be using Expo to develop an app for Android next.

Developing for Android

If you want to develop and test an Expo app on Android, you will need to either connect your Android device to your computer (with **Developer** and **Debugging** modes enabled) or set up a virtual device with Android Studio first. If you don't have an Android device, you will need to first install Android Studio with this link: https://developer. android.com/studio. After the installation, open Android Studio, go to **Tools | AVD Manager**, and select **Create Virtual Device**.

Choose an emulator device on the following screen, based on either the device you own or the desirable resolution that you would want to use to build your app:

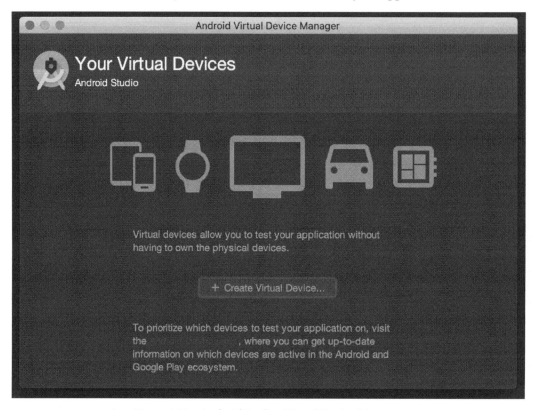

Figure 1.12 – Android Studio: Virtual Device Manager

I would recommend choosing a device with the highest resolution and density to ensure your graphical elements are prepared for these devices. Since I actually own a Nexus 6 and it has the highest resolution (screen resolution 1,440x2,960) and density (pixel density 560 **dots per inch** (**dpi**)), I selected **Nexus 6** as the emulator for development. Nexus 6 is still capable of running an Android 10 OS, which is why I do not yet need to buy any new Android devices for development. For those who do not own an Android device and aren't planning to buy one for development, you could choose the **Pixel 3 XL** option for now, as illustrated in the following screenshot. If you need to test the Google Play API services, then you could always install an additional device such as Pixel:

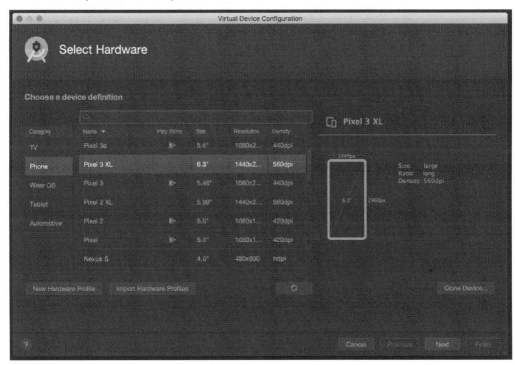

Figure 1.13 – Virtual Device Configuration – Selecting a device

Once you hit **Next**, you will be asked to choose a system image, as follows:

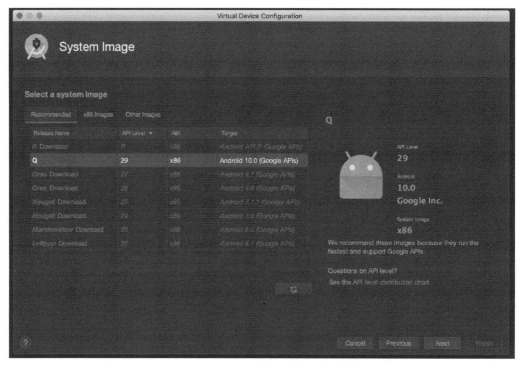

Figure 1.14 – Virtual Device Configuration: Selecting a system image

By default, Android Studio pre-selects the **x86 Android Q** image with Google APIs support. If you want to change that for whatever reason, such as developing for the next-gen Android R OS, click on the **x86 Images** tab and then choose the x86_64 image with **Android API R (Google APIs)** as the target, as illustrated in the following screenshot. Since Android R might not be installed by default, you have to click the **Download** button to download the Android R image before you can click **Next** to go on to the next step:

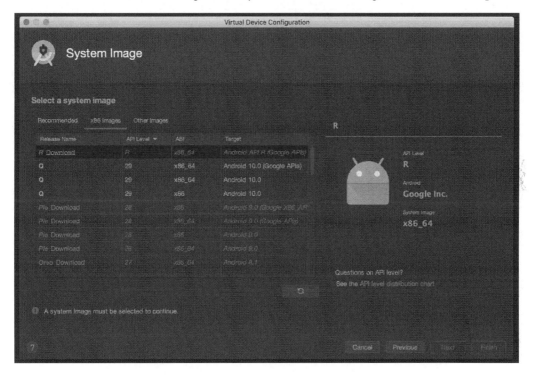

Figure 1.15 – Virtual Device Configuration: Selecting an x86_64 system image

Once you have decided on your emulator and system image (in my case, I've selected **Nexus 6** with **Android 10.0 x86**), you will see the following screen, which lets you rename the **Android Virtual Device (AVD)**. Let's click on the **Show Advanced Settings** button:

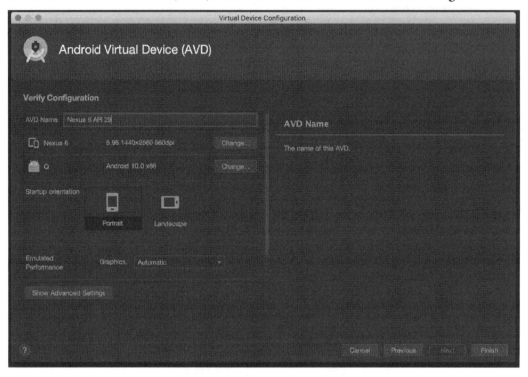

Figure 1.16 – Virtual Device Configuration: Verify the Configuration

As you can see on the following screen, the front camera is set to **Emulated** by default and the back camera is disabled, which is not what we want during development if our app needs to use the cameras on the phone:

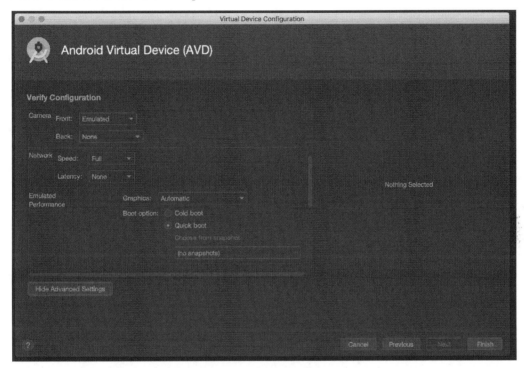

Figure 1.17 – Virtual Device Configuration: Advanced Settings

Since you might want to actually test the camera quickly during development, you can choose Webcam0 for both front and back camera if your development machine has a webcam installed (otherwise, you can choose **Emulated** for both the front and back cameras). If you don't need to use the camera for your app, you can just leave the setting as is.

In the **Emulated Performance** section, leave the **Graphics** setting as **Automatic** to let the emulator allocate resources automatically. But on the **Boot option** part, we have to choose the **Cold boot** option in **Advanced Settings** to avoid running into the well-known `Can't find service:` `package` error in Expo (there is a link to the issue on GitHub, at `https://github.com/facebook/react-native/issues/24725`). You can leave the rest of **Advanced Settings** at their default settings because they are based on the actual device settings, unless you want to squeeze more performance out of your development machine, in which case you are free to select more **central processing unit (CPU)** core and memory allocation, which should be very straightforward so we won't cover it here. Just click **Finish** on the following screen:

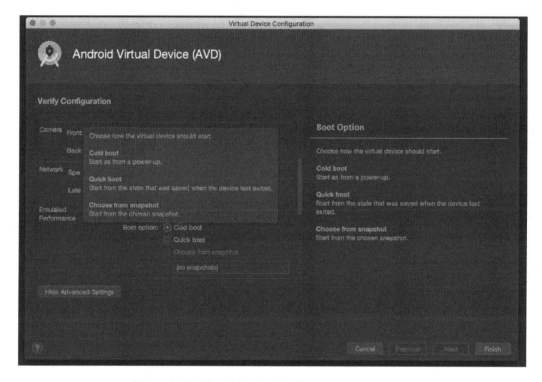

Figure 1.18 – Virtual Device Configuration: Boot option

You should now be able to see the new emulator device being created in the **Your Virtual Devices** list and the device selection on the emulator dropdown at the top. You can always install more emulators by yourself later if you want to cover more devices for testing. Since Android has a huge fragmentation on screen resolution and pixel density as well as running OSes on the market, it makes sense to test on different emulators and OSes during development. If you want to change the settings for whatever reason, you can always click the little pen icon to edit the settings, as illustrated in the following screenshot:

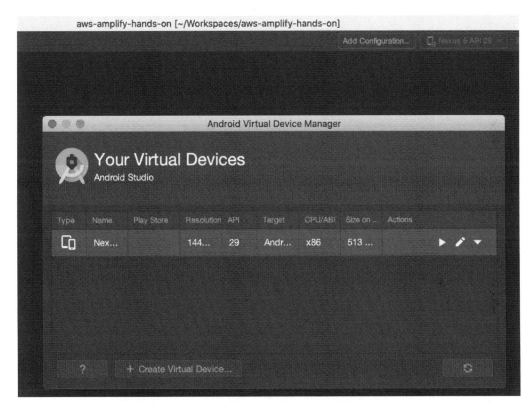

Figure 1.19 – Virtual Device Configuration: Camera settings

Now, go back to Terminal or the terminal of your code editor and run the following command:

```
yarn android
```

You should be able to see the following screen if everything worked as expected:

Open up App.tsx to start working on your app!

Figure 1.20 – Android emulator

Since the screen is asking you to open up the App.tsx file on your project to start working on your app, you can go ahead and edit the App.tsx file and save it (*Command + S* on a Mac or *Ctrl + S* on a PC/Linux). You should then be able to see that the app has changed accordingly in real time on the Android emulator to confirm it is working, as illustrated in the following screenshot:

Figure 1.21 – Running the Expo app in the Android emulator

Important note

If you still encounter the `Can't find service: package` error even with the **Cold boot** option of **Advanced Settings**, as in the Expo CLI not being able to install and run the new build package on the Android emulator, the reason could be that the Expo client has not been installed properly on the Android emulator. If that happens, you can shut down the emulator with the **Power** button and press *A* on the keyboard to rerun the Android emulator in the terminal, which will trigger the Expo client installation for the Android emulator. Once the Expo client is being installed locally, turn on the emulator again and see if the Expo app is installed or not. Now, you can rerun the `yarn android` command to run the app on the Android emulator with the Expo client.

Developing for the web

Run the following command to run the Expo app as a web app in the browser:

```
yarn web
```

You should be able to see the following screen if everything worked as expected:

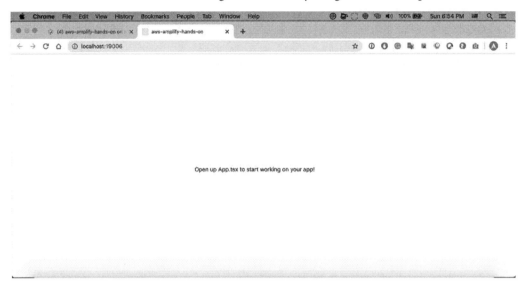

Figure 1.22 – Running the Expo app on a browser

Since the screen is asking you to open up the App.tsx file in your project to start working on your app, you can go ahead and edit the App.tsx file and save it (*Command + S* on a Mac or *Ctrl + S* on a PC/Linux). You should then be able to see that the app has changed accordingly in real time in the browser to confirm it is working, as illustrated in the following screenshot:

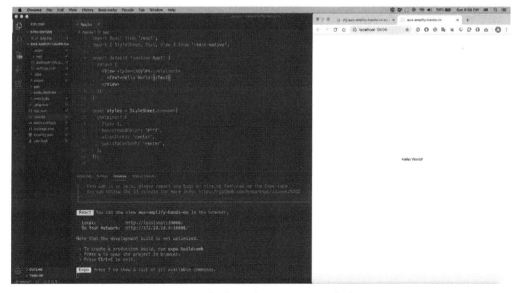

Figure 1.23 – Refreshing the Expo app in the browser

> **Important note**
>
> At the time of writing this book, web support is out of the box but it is still in beta, which means some of the components are not fully supported for the web yet.

Now that you are familiar with how to create a new app with the Expo CLI, we will discover how to create a **Progressive Web App** (**PWA**) with React in the next section.

Creating a new PWA

If you are planning on developing your Amplify app with React for the web only or you are planning to write the React Native code separately, creating a pure React app makes much more sense. You can run the following command to create a React app with TypeScript:

```
yarn create react-app my-app-name --template typescript
```

Once you have created your React PWA with TypeScript, here are a few commands to remember:

Command	Description
yarn start	Starts the development server
yarn build	Bundles the app into static files for production
yarn test	Starts the test runner

You should be able to see the following screen when you run the `yarn start` command:

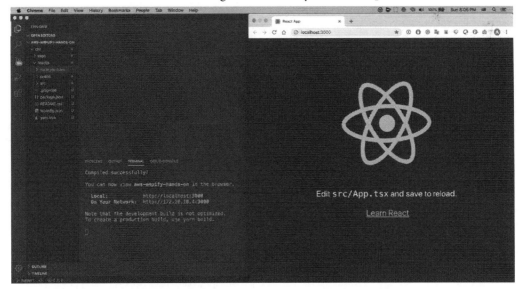

Figure 1.24 – Running the ReactJS app in a browser

Change something in the App.tsx file and save it (*Command + S* on a Mac or *Ctrl + S* on a PC/Linux). You should then be able to see that the app has changed accordingly in real time in the browser to confirm it is working, as illustrated in the following screenshot:

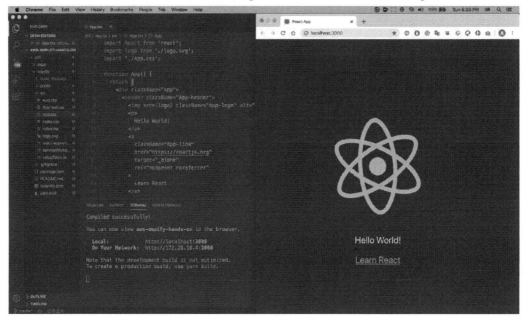

Figure 1.25 – Updating the ReactJS app in the browser

If you run the `yarn build` command, you will see a `build` folder being created, as illustrated in the following screenshot. You can upload the `build` folder to your web server or AWS S3 bucket as static web hosting to see it working in production, which we will cover later in this book:

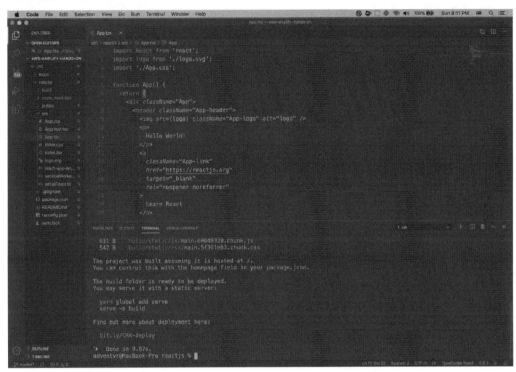

Figure 1.26 – Creating the ReactJS app folder

If you run the `yarn test` command, you will see the `App.test.tsx` script being executed to test against the `App.tsx` file. The console will tell you how many tests have been run and how many have passed, as illustrated in the following screenshot:

Figure 1.27 – Passing the unit test of the ReactJS app

It is important to know that the `test` command will watch the changes of the directory as well as the `start` command, so any changes to the repository will trigger the test again. You can always use the command the terminal suggested to run the test in different ways, as follows:

Command	Description
Press *A* on keyboard	Run all tests again
Press *F* on keyboard	Run only failed test again
Press *Q* on keyboard	Quit Watch mode
Press *P* on keyboard	Filter tests by filename with regular expression
Press *T* on keyboard	Filter tests by test name with regular expression
Press *Enter* on keyboard	Trigger a test run, which is same as a
Press *Ctrl* + *C* on keyboard	Quit the test

Now that you are familiar with how to build a React app with TypeScript, we will go through how to create a React Native app with the React Native CLI in the next section.

Creating a new React Native app

If you have a Mac and you want to create a React Native app without Expo or you want to support a platform such as macOS or Windows in the future, you can use the React Native CLI to create one. In order to build a React Native app, we need to install a few dependencies, such as Node.js, Watchman (Watchman is a tool by Facebook for watching changes in the filesystem), Xcode command-line tools, and CocoaPods (CocoaPods is a dependency manager for Swift and Objective-C Cocoa projects). You can use the following commands to install the dependencies and create a React Native app with TypeScript:

```
brew install node
brew install watchman
xcode-select --install
sudo gem install cocoapods
npx react-native init MyApp --template react-native-template-
typescript
```

Once you have created your React Native app with the React Native CLI, here are a few commands to remember:

Command	Description
yarn ios	Run the iOS app in the iOS simulator.
yarn android	Run the Android app in the Android emulator. If you run into any issues here, you can always go back to the previous *Developing for Android* section to set up Android Studio and the AVD first.
yarn test	Run all Jest unit tests.
yarn lint	Analyze the code for potential errors and warnings.

When you run the `yarn ios` command, the React Native CLI will build the iOS app and then launch the iOS simulator. Once the build is done, the React Native CLI will launch the Metro builder in the terminal and then launch the React Native app, as shown in the following screenshot:

Figure 1.28 – Running the iOS React Native app

The Metro builder is working with the native iOS app in the simulator simultaneously in order to push the build result to the app as soon as there are new changes. Change something in the App.tsx file and save it (*Command + S* on a Mac or *Ctrl + S* on a PC/ Linux). You should then be able to see that the app has changed accordingly in real time in the iOS simulator, as illustrated in the following screenshot:

Figure 1.29 – Updating the iOS React Native app

If you run the `yarn android` command while leaving the iOS simulator and the Metro builder open in the terminal, you will see the Android app being built and launched with the Android emulator. When you make changes in the `App.tsx` file, you will see changes being updated on both virtual devices simultaneously, as shown here:

Figure 1.30 – Running both an iOS and an Android React Native app

You have now created at least one—or several—React and React Native apps if you followed the instructions in this chapter. You should now be familiar with the different CLIs and ways to create React and React Native apps.

Summary

You should now have a basic understanding of how to integrate or start an AWS Amplify project with React and React Native using TypeScript. It is important to understand the fundamentals and the options when creating your project with different React and Amplify CLIs, because your next project might have very specific requirements and you will want to start the project in the right way, without too many changes down the road.

Since React, React Native, and Expo are under rapid development and keep adding new capabilities every month, if you want to keep your knowledge up to date, you should always follow their websites closely to learn of all the new changes and apply them to your project accordingly. When I was halfway through the writing of this chapter, AWS completely changed the way the AWS Amplify UI works with their new library, which we will cover in the next chapter. Therefore, timing matters. If you are halfway through your project or are just starting a new project, it would be worthwhile us going through the next chapter together to see how to create an AWS Amplify app with the latest pre-built Amplify UI.

2
Creating a React App with AmplifyJS and TypeScript

Now that we've familiarized ourselves with the Amplify CLI and Amplify Console, in this chapter, we will build a simple to-do app with **TypeScript** (**TS**) without writing much code. The idea is for you to get used to transitioning to TypeScript if you have not used it already. TypeScript is based on the concept of Strongly Typed, which means you can avoid a lot of runtime errors compared to using **JavaScript** (**JS**). This is because the transpiler (TS will get transpiled into JS, so it is not a compiler) will give you errors and warnings during transpilation when the types don't match.

The main reason we're following this to-do example is to give you an idea of how quickly we can build a basic React app with data input, store and retrieve data on DynamoDB, create the latest API 4.0 (GraphQL), and use **Function as a Service** (**FaaS**) and NoOps. That is all you need to create your next interactive prototype for user testing or hackathons. This chapter will show you how to build a skeleton app so that you can build and test your next big idea. We will cover the following topics:

- Creating a new project with React or React Native with TypeScript
- Setting up the backend

- Adding an API with GraphQL and DynamoDB

- Integrating the GraphQL API with the ReactJS app

- Launching the ReactJS app

Technical requirements

This chapter requires that you have completed the exercises in *Chapter 1, Getting Familiar with the Amplify CLI and Amplify Console*. You can download the code for this chapter from the following link: `https://github.com/PacktPublishing/Rapid-Application-Development-with-AWS-Amplify/tree/master/ch2`.

> **Important Note**
>
> It is important that you keep your libraries up to date if you want to have better compatibility with the latest browsers and mobile operating systems, such as iOS and Android OS. Run the `yarn upgrade` command to keep your app up to date once in a while.

Creating a new project with React or React Native with TypeScript

I am glad that both React and React Native actually share the exact same processes for adding AWS Amplify to existing projects. Now, let's add the AWS Amplify library and Amplify UI to our app.

Installing AWS Amplify dependencies

Before we dive into the details of how to create the to-do list app and connect it to the backend, we will need to add the necessary dependencies to our projects:

1. For the ReactJS project, enter the following command:

    ```
    ? yarn add aws-amplify @aws-amplify/ui-react
    ```

2. For the Expo project, enter the following command:

    ```
    yarn add aws-amplify aws-amplify-react-native @react-native-community/netinfo
    ```

For the React Native project, things are more complicated. We need to follow these steps:

1. Enter the following command:

```
yarn add aws-amplify aws-amplify-react-native amazon-
cognito-identity-js react-native-vector-icons @react-
native-community/netinfo
```

2. Run the following command to link the dependencies:

```
npx react-native link
```

3. (Optional) For Mac and iOS only, go to the iOS folder and then install the pod dependencies:

```
cd ios && pod install
```

4. (Optional) Go back to the root folder of the project:

```
cd ..
```

Now, we should be ready to start integrating AWS Amplify into our project.

Setting up the backend

Now that you have installed the AWS Amplify dependencies, you will need to initialize the project by running the `amplify init` command in your terminal. You will run into a series of questions that will help you choose the right settings for your project. In our case, we only need to press *Enter* to choose the default prompted answers and wait for the process to complete. Here is an example of the React Native project after running the `amplify init` command:

```
? Enter a name for the project reactnative
? Enter a name for the environment dev
? Choose your default editor: Visual Studio Code
? Choose the type of app that you're building javascript
Please tell us about your project
? What javascript framework are you using react-native
? Source Directory Path:  /
? Distribution Directory Path: /
? Build Command:  npm run-script build
? Start Command: npm run-script start
```

```
Using default provider  awscloudformation

For more information on AWS Profiles, see:

https://docs.aws.amazon.com/cli/latest/userguide/cli-multiple-
profiles.html

? Do you want to use an AWS profile? Yes

? Please choose the profile you want to use default
```

Once the Amplify CLI initiation process is complete, you will see the following message in the Terminal:

```
√ Successfully created initial AWS cloud resources for
deployments.

√ Initialized provider successfully.

Initialized your environment successfully.

Your project has been successfully initialized and connected to
the cloud!

Some next steps:

"amplify status" will show you what you've added already and if
it's locally configured or deployed

"amplify add <category>" will allow you to add features like
user login or a backend API

"amplify push" will build all your local backend resources and
provision it in the cloud

"amplify console" to open the Amplify Console and view your
project status

"amplify publish" will build all your local backend and
frontend resources (if you have hosting category added) and
provision it in the cloud

Pro tip:

Try "amplify add api" to create a backend API and then "amplify
publish" to deploy everything
```

The preceding code explains a few things you can do next, which we mentioned in *Chapter 1, Getting Familiar with the Amplify CLI and Amplify Console,* such as adding an API and publishing the app. We are going to add the GraphQL API and connect it to DynamoDB in the next section. Most modern applications still use the RESTful API instead of the GraphQL API, which slows down the development process because of the complexity of having multiple endpoints, schemas, and data structures. GraphQL standardized the schema syntax, data types, and query structure, and also reduced using multiple endpoints into just one single endpoint.

Adding an API with GraphQL and DynamoDB

Now, let's add the GraphQL API to the app by running the `amplify add api` command in a Terminal. We will choose a to-do list template as the example for this chapter:

```
? amplify add api
? Please select from one of the below mentioned services:
GraphQL
? Provide API name: my-api-name
? Choose the default authorization type for the API: API key
? Enter a description for the API key: dev
? After how many days from now the API key should expire (1-
365): 365
? Do you want to configure advanced settings for the GraphQL
API? No, I am done.
? Do you have an annotated GraphQL schema? No
? Choose a schema template: Single object with fields (e.g.,
"Todo" with ID, name, description)
? Do you want to edit the schema now? Yes
```

Before we modify the code, we should call the `amplify push` command to trigger the code generator. This will generate the GraphQL code first:

```
? amplify push
? Do you want to generate code for your newly created GraphQL
API: Yes
? Choose the code generation language target: typescript
? Enter the file name pattern of graphql queries, mutations and
subscriptions src/graphql/**/*.ts
? Do you want to generate/update all possible GraphQL
operations - queries, mutations and subscriptions Yes
? Enter maximum statement depth [increase from default if your
schema is deeply nested] 2
? Enter the file name for the generated code src/API.ts
√ Generated GraphQL operations successfully and saved at
   src/graphql
√ Code generated successfully and saved in file src/API.ts
√ All resources are updated in the cloud
GraphQL endpoint: https://xxxxx.appsync-api.us-east-1.
```

```
amazonaws.com/graphql
GraphQL API KEY: xxxxx
```

The GraphQL code has been generated in the `src` folder, and the endpoint and API key can be reused between your ReactJS, Expo, and React Native projects. So, please keep the endpoint and API key details somewhere safe.

Let's go through a few files that the generator has created and discuss what they are:

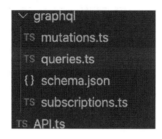

Figure 2.1 – Viewing the generated code files in Visual Studio Code

The `API.ts` file is the key interface we can use to interact with the GraphQL API. It has generated type objects for us to call so that we can fetch or modify data on DynamoDB. `schema.json` is a file that contains the GraphQL schema and tells us how we are supposed to interact with the GraphQL API. The most important concepts that we need to learn about here are **queries**, **mutations**, and **subscriptions**. In simple terms, queries help us fetch data, mutations help us modify data in the database, and subscriptions help us listen to changes in the data so that we can display them to the user.

The generated JavaScript code blocks do not have any ending semi-colons, `;`. This is an ES5 (Ecma-262 Edition 5.1, The ECMAScript Language Specification in June 2011) feature called **Automatic Semicolon Insertion** (**ASI**). Many people prefer not writing semi-colons and letting ES5 take care of it with ASI. But I want to point out here that semi-colons improve readability; it's the same as adding a full stop to the end of a sentence. It acts as a sign that tells you where the code should have ended. It is important to have an indicator, even though some people might argue that we could change the TypeScript settings to enable the not unexpected-multiline feature in the settings. But what if the code was ported to a new project or merged with somebody else's code without this setting? In those edge cases, without semi-colons, this could break your code, with unintended consequences.

Let's open the `App.tsx` file. As you can see, the sample code of the to-do list app has been generated with JavaScript. It contains a lot of errors when we open it up as part of the TypeScript project. I will break down the code into smaller chunks and explain it in the following sections.

Integrating the GraphQL API with the ReactJS app

For the ReactJS project, we must open the `App.tsx` file under the `src` folder to look at the JavaScript code that was generated by the Amplify CLI. Then, we must change the TypeScript code, as follows:

1. The following code was generated without any semi-colons. We will add them back in the TypeScript version. This code imports the essential libraries for React, Amplify, and GraphQL:

    ```
    import React, { useEffect, useState } from 'react'
    import Amplify, { API, graphqlOperation } from
    'aws-amplify'
    import { createTodo } from './graphql/mutations'
    import { listTodos } from './graphql/queries'
    ```

2. The following code block imports your AWS account settings and your own credentials. These have been marked so that they not submitted to GitHub. This is because your credentials are supposed to be private to everyone. Therefore, if someone needs to pull from your repository, they need to set up their own IAM credentials again with the Amplify CLI:

    ```
    import awsExports from "./aws-exports";
    Amplify.configure(awsExports);
    ```

3. The following code block shows us how to use the `State` Hook (https://reactjs.org/docs/hooks-state.html). Since React version 16.8, the initial state is set to an object with a variable called `name` and a string as its value. Feel free to change the string to something else to see how it works. The `todos` and `setTodos` objects are set to be empty arrays, which means they have been initialized and are ready for you to add some items to them:

    ```
    const initialState = { name: '', description: '' }

    const App = () => {
      const [formState, setFormState] =
      useState(initialState)
      const [todos, setTodos] = useState([])
    ```

4. The following code block shows you how to use the `Effect` Hook (`https://reactjs.org/docs/hooks-effect.html`). The `Effect` Hook is meant to be used for subscribing to events. In this case, we are subscribing to the component changing. When we call the `fetchTodos` method, it fetches data into the `todos` array; the frontend code will render the items within the `todos` array in the browser. Therefore, it will trigger the `fetchTodos` method with the `useEffect` Hook:

```
useEffect(() => {
    fetchTodos()
}, [])
```

5. The following code block shows the `setInput` and `fetchTodos` methods:

```
function setInput(key, value) {
    setFormState({ ...formState, [key]: value })
}

async function fetchTodos() {
    try {
        const todoData = await
        API.graphql(graphqlOperation(listTodos))
        const todos = todoData.data.listTodos.items
        setTodos(todos)
    } catch (err) { console.log('error fetching todos') }
}
```

6. The following code block shows you how to use the `addTodo` method:

```
async function addTodo() {
    try {
        if (!formState.name || !formState.description)
    return
        const todo = { ...formState }
        setTodos([...todos, todo])
        setFormState(initialState)
        await API.graphql(graphqlOperation(createTodo,
    {input:
```

```
            todo}))
        } catch (err) {
        console.log('error creating todo:', err)
        }
    }
```

7. The following code block shows the `return` section of the component itself, which is the HTML code for rendering the **User Interface** (**UI**):

```
return (
    <div style={styles.container}>
        <h2>Amplify Todos</h2>
        <input
            onChange={event => setInput('name',
            event.target.value)}
            style={styles.input}
            value={formState.name}
            placeholder="Name"
        />
        <input
            onChange={event => setInput('description',
            event.target.value)}
            style={styles.input}
            value={formState.description}
            placeholder="Description"
        />
        <button style={styles.button}
        onClick={addTodo}>Create
        Todo</button>
        {
            todos.map((todo, index) => (
                <div key={todo.id ? todo.id : index}
                style={styles.todo}>
                    <p style={styles.todoName}>{todo.name}</p>
                    <p style={styles.todoDescription}>
                    {todo.description}</p>
```

```
            </div>
        ))
    }
    </div>
    )
}
```

8. The following code block shows you the inline styling of the HTML UI elements:

```
const styles = {
    container: { width: 400, margin: '0 auto', display:
    'flex',
    flex: 1, flexDirection: 'column', justifyContent:
    'center',
    padding: 20 },
    todo: {  marginBottom: 15 },
    input: { border: 'none', backgroundColor: '#ddd',
    marginBottom: 10, padding: 8, fontSize: 18 },
    todoName: { fontSize: 20, fontWeight: 'bold' },
    todoDescription: { marginBottom: 0 },
    button: { backgroundColor: 'black', color: 'white',
    outline:
    'none', fontSize: 18, padding: '12px 0px' }
}
```

9. The following code block shows you how to export the reusable and importable App object, which you can call from other classes, such as index.tsx:

```
export default App
```

As you can see, we have a lot of type errors in the default example code:

Figure 2.2 – TypeScript (TS) type errors based on the JavaScript (JS) sample code

10. Now, go ahead and edit the App.tsx file. Then, change the JS syntax into TS syntax, as shown in the following code:

```
import React, { useEffect, useState, SetStateAction }
from 'react';
import './App.css';


import Amplify, { API, graphqlOperation } from
'aws-amplify';
import { createTodo } from './graphql/mutations';
import { listTodos } from './graphql/queries';


import awsExports from "./aws-exports";
Amplify.configure(awsExports);


const initialState = { name: '', description: '' };
const App = () => {
  const [formState, setFormState] =
  useState(initialState);
  const [todos, setTodos] = useState([]);

```

```
useEffect (() => {
    fetchTodos ();
}, []);
```

After adding a semi-colon to the end of each line, we must import App.css.
This is because we are going to be externalizing the styles into a **Cascading Style Sheet** (**CSS**) file.

11. Change the setInput function to const with the new arrow operator
(https://www.typescriptlang.org/docs/handbook/functions.
html). We will need to add a return type to the method. In our case, we will add
any because it allows anything in TypeScript that is considered to be a wildcard
return type:

```
const setInput = (key: any, value: any):any => {
    setFormState({ ...formState, [key]: value });
}
```

12. Any async method should return Promise with a preferable type:

```
const fetchTodos = async (): Promise<any> => {
  try {
    const todoData:any = await
    API.graphql (graphqlOperation (listTodos));
    const todos:any = todoData.data.listTodos.items;
    setTodos (todos);
  } catch (err) {
    console.log('error fetching todos');
  }
}

const addTodo = async (): Promise<any> => {
  try {
    if (!formState.name || !formState.description)
return;
    const todo = { ...formState };
```

13. If we know that the actual type of the input object is as follows, we can use the `as` syntax to cast the array object into the right strongly typed array object, called `SetStateAction<never[]>`:

```
    setTodos([...todos, todo] as
    SetStateAction<never[]>);
    setFormState(initialState);
    await API.graphql(graphqlOperation(createTodo,
{input:
    todo}));
    } catch (err) {
    console.log('error creating todo:', err);
    }
  }
```

14. Because we have externalized the inline styling to the `App.css` file, we can add the CSS class with a name:

```
  return (
    <div className="container">
      <h2>Amplify Todos</h2>
      <input
        onChange={event => setInput('name',
        event.target.value)}
        value={formState.name}
        placeholder="Name"
      />
      <input
        onChange={event => setInput('description',
        event.target.value)}
        value={formState.description}
        placeholder="Description"
      />
      <button onClick={addTodo}>Create Todo</button>
      {
        todos.map((todo: any, index: any) => (
          <div key={todo.id ? todo.id : index}
          className="todo">
```

```
          <p className="todoName">{todo.name}</p>
          <p className="todoDescription">
          {todo.description}</p>
        </div>
      ))
    }
    </div>
  )
}

export default App
```

15. Edit the new App.css file with the following code. As you can see, you can use the universal CSS styling syntax here instead of the React styling syntax, which makes more sense to frontend developers:

```
.container {
  width: 400px;
  margin: 0 auto;
  display: flex;
  flex: 1;
  flex-direction: column;
  justify-content: center;
  padding: 20px;
}

.todo {
  margin-bottom: 15px;
}

input {
  border: none;
  background-color: #ddd;
  margin-bottom: 10px;
  padding: 8px;
  font-size: 18px;
}
```

16. Make sure that you are adding semi-colons at the end of each line:

```
.todoName {
    font-size: 20px;
    font-weight: bold;
}

.todoDescription {
    margin-bottom: 0;
}

button {
    background-color: black;
    color: white;
    outline: none;
    font-size: 18px;
    padding: 12px 0px;
}
```

You might have noticed that we moved the hardcoded inline CSS that was generated as part of the to-do list example by the CLI to the external CSS file. Now, you can write CSS with standard CSS syntax instead of React-specific inline CSS. CSS is supposed to be reusable and extendable. Therefore, externalizing the CSS instead of hardcoding it as inline CSS would be more maintainable and reusable. In the next section, we will host our app with Amplify Hosting and launch it in the browser with an URL.

Launching the ReactJS app

Let's call the `amplify add hosting` command to integrate all our code with Amplify Hosting. This will allow us to host the app with a dedicated URL so that we can share it with our friends or customers for user testing. Let's get started:

1. Go back to your Terminal and enter the `amplify add hosting` command to configure Amplify Hosting through the Amplify CLI:

```
amplify add hosting
Select the plugin module to execute (Use arrow keys)
> Hosting with Amplify Console (Managed hosting with
```

```
custom domains, Continuous deployment)
  Amazon CloudFront and S3
Choose a type
  Continuous deployment (Git-based deployments)
> Manual deployment
You can now publish your app using the following command:
amplify publish
```

2. Use the arrow keys to select **manual deployment**. Then, run the amplify publish command to publish the artifacts to the development environment with a staging URL:

```
✓ Successfully pulled backend environment dev from the cloud.
? Are you sure you want to continue? Yes
⁚ Updating resources in the cloud. This may take a few minutes...
✓ All resources are updated in the cloud
Creating an optimized production build...
Compiled successfully.
✓ Zipping artifacts completed.
✓ Deployment complete!
https://dev.xxxxx.amplifyapp.com
```

3. Open the staging URL in the browser that is generated by the Amplify CLI. We will see that the to-do list app is up and running, as shown in the following screenshot:

Figure 2.3 – Running the to-do list app on a browser

4. Let's test the app by entering the **name** and **description** details of the to-do list item and then hitting *Enter*:

Figure 2.4 – Testing the to-do list app in a browser

As soon as we click the **Create Todo** button, we should be able to see the progressive web app being updated, as follows:

Figure 2.5 – Checking the test result of the to-do list app in a browser

The reason why the to-do list is being updated is because the code uses the *Effect Hook* (Hooks are a new addition to React 16.8) to trigger the *fetch todo list* query. Therefore, as soon as the React app updates the DOM, the `Effect` Hook will trigger the `fetchTodos` method:

```
useEffect(() => {
    fetchTodos();
}, []);
```

Figure 2.6 – The useEffect method will call the fetchTodos method

Now, let's go to the DynamoDB home page (`https://console.aws.amazon.com/dynamodb/home`) to find out what's going on behind the scenes. As we can see, it stored the data in DynamoDB:

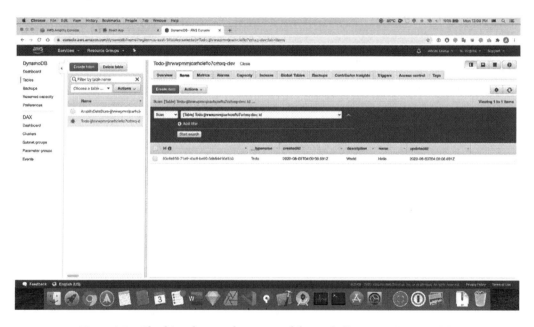

Figure 2.7 – Checking the new data entry of the to-do list app in DynamoDB

With that, we have successfully created and stored the data in DynamoDB as a record with a unique ID and timestamps. It's just that easy! You are well on your way to creating the next big thing.

Integrating the GraphQL API with the React Native and Expo apps

For the Expo and React Native projects, we cannot use standard CSS; we must use the React way of styling. If you want to let the user switch between light and dark modes on your app, you must keep the styling for the external files so that you can use code to switch between the different themes. In this case, we will create the AppStyles.ts file in the root directory with the following code:

```
import { StyleSheet } from 'react-native';

export default StyleSheet.create({
    container: { flex: 1, justifyContent: 'center', padding: 20
},
    todo: { marginBottom: 15 },
    input: { height: 50, backgroundColor: '#ddd', marginBottom:
    10,
    padding: 8 },
    todoName: { fontSize: 18 }
});
```

Now, we will open the App.tsx file and add the following code blocks:

1. Import the necessary React libraries:

```
import React, { useEffect, useState, SetStateAction }
from 'react';
```

2. Import the React Native components for both the Expo and React Native projects:

```
import { View, Text, TextInput, Button } from 'react-
native';
```

3. Import the AppStyles file, which we are going to create soon:

```
import styles from './AppStyles';
import Amplify, { API, graphqlOperation } from
'aws-amplify';
import { createTodo } from './src/graphql/mutations';
import { listTodos } from './src/graphql/queries';
```

4. Import the AWS settings for the Expo project only. We will need to change `aws-exports.js` to `aws-exports.ts` to avoid any import errors:

```
import awsExports from "./aws-exports";
Amplify.configure(awsExports);
```

5. As you can see, the following code blocks are pretty much the same as they are for the ReactJS project, which means that most of the code between ReactJS, Expo, and React Native can be reused if we code it carefully, This includes the way we write `useState` with the any array type to avoid TypeScript errors. If you want to keep things consistent between the ReactJS project and the Expo or ReactNative project, you can do the following:

```
const initialState = { name: '', description: '' }

const App = () => {
  const [formState, setFormState] =
  useState(initialState);
  const [todos, setTodos] = useState<any[]>([]);

  useEffect(() => {
    fetchTodos();
  }, []);
```

6. For normal functions, we will convert them into a `const` type with a return type of any:

```
const setInput = (key: any, value: any):any => {
  setFormState({ ...formState, [key]: value });
}
```

7. For `async` functions, we will convert them into a `const` type with a return type of `Promise<any>`:

```
const fetchTodos = async (): Promise<any> => {
  try {
    const todoData:any = await
    API.graphql(graphqlOperation(listTodos));
    const todos:any = todoData.data.listTodos.items;
    setTodos(todos);
```

```
    } catch (err) {
        console.log('error fetching todos');
    }
  }


  const addTodo = async (): Promise<any> => {
    try {
        if (!formState.name || !formState.description)
  return;
        const todo = { ...formState };
        setTodos([...todos, todo] as
        SetStateAction<any[]>);
        setFormState(initialState);
        await API.graphql(graphqlOperation(createTodo,
{input:
        todo}));
    } catch (err) {
        console.log('error creating todo:', err);
    }
  }
```

8. For React Native and Expo, the base components are not generic HTML components but React Native components. If we want to keep the code similar to the ReactJS project's, we must create the base component so that it has the same name as the React Native component. For example, we can create a `View` component instead of using `Div` for ReactJS. In this case, we will use the React Native component. I believe this is exactly why Expo supports the web–to help developers avoid creating multiple versions of the same React projects and for maintaining two different code bases. This is because Expo can actually run and build the project for the web:

```
    return (
        <View style={styles.container}>
          <TextInput
            onChangeText={val => setInput('name', val)}
            style={styles.input}
            value={formState.name}
            placeholder="Name"
```

```
    />
    <TextInput
      onChangeText={val => setInput('description',
      val)}
      style={styles.input}
      value={formState.description}
      placeholder="Description"
    />
    <Button title="Create Todo" onPress={addTodo} />
    {
      todos.map((todo, index) => (
        <View key={todo.id ? todo.id : index}
        style={styles.todo}>
          <Text style={styles.todoName}>{todo.name}</
          Text>
          <Text>{todo.description}</Text>
        </View>
      ))
    }
    </View>
  )
}

export default App
```

With that, we have created the to-do app and connected the Expo and React Native projects to the GraphQL backend. Now, we must test the app to see if it runs on different devices.

Launching the React Native and Expo apps

For the Expo project, we will test the web, iOS, and Android versions:

1. Let's test out the web version first by entering the yarn web command in a Terminal:

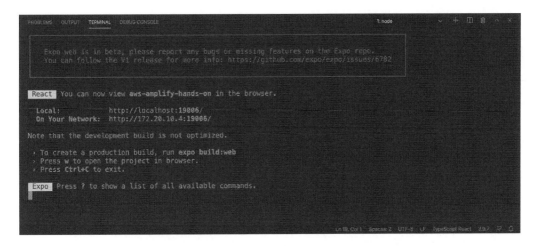

Figure 2.8 – The Expo CLI will show you the local URL and open it in your browser

2. A browser will open. It will start the metro builder and compile the web version of the app:

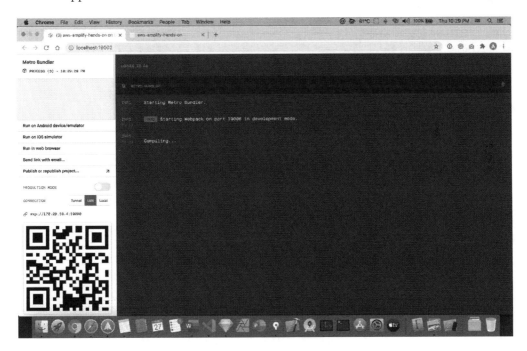

Figure 2.9 – Compiling the web version of the app

3. Once the compilation is complete, a new tab will open in your browser automatically. You will see that the app is running, as shown in the following screenshot:

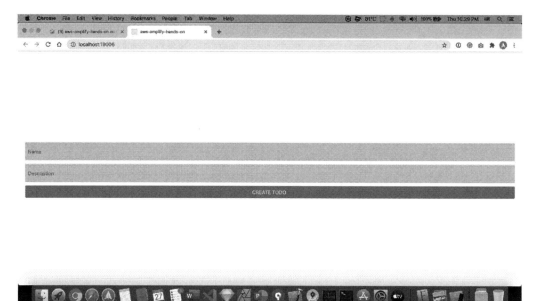

Figure 2.10 – The Expo to-do app running in a browser

As you can see, the styling of the Expo and React Native apps has been optimized for mobile, so the button and the input fields have been stretched across the screen. If you want to make this look nicer, you can add a fixed width for the button and input fields. Let's press *Ctrl + C* in our Terminal to end the Expo CLI process and try out the iOS and Android versions of it.

For iOS and Mac users, if you are on a Mac with Xcode installed, you can run the `yarn ios` command; you will see that the app is running on the iOS simulator. It will run the method builder dashboard in the browser and show you a couple of options for running the app. From the left menu, you will see the **Run on Android device/emulator**, **Run on iOS simulator**, and **Run in web browser** buttons. You can press these buttons and rerun the app on different virtual devices at any time. In this case, we can see that the iOS version of the app is running successfully:

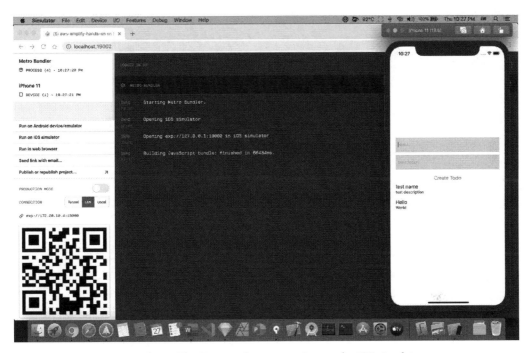

Figure 2.11 – The Expo to-do app running on the iOS simulator

For Android users, if you have Android Studio installed, you can run the `yarn android` command in a Terminal:

1. As you can see, the Expo CLI is telling you that you can switch between different virtual devices at any time by pressing different keys on your keyboard. Pressing *A* will run the app on the Android emulator, pressing *I* will run the app on the iOS simulator, and pressing *W* will run the app in your web browser:

Figure 2.12 – The Expo CLI showing different app running options

2. However, sometimes, the Android version of the app won't start initially due to a cold boot issue. This means it will run into a **Couldn't start project on Android** error. To amend this, you need to shut down the Android emulator by pressing the **power** button and then press it again to turn it back on. After that, press the **Run on Android device/emulator** button on your browser:

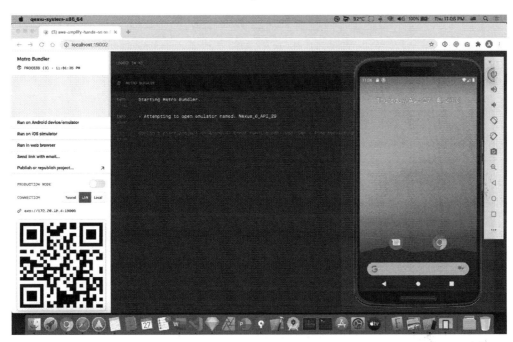

Figure 2.13 – The known cold start issue

3.   Now, the Android version of the Expo app should be running, as follows:

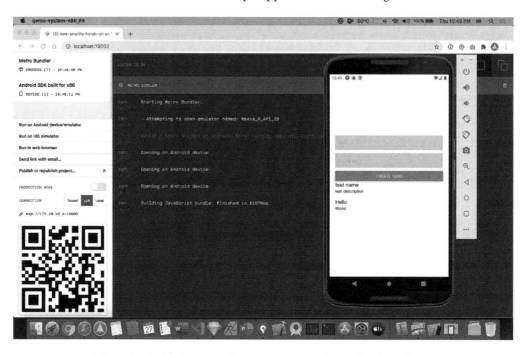

Figure 2.14 – The Expo to-do app running on the Android emulator

So, the Expo version of the to-do app is running perfectly on all platforms. Let's do the same for the React Native app. Run the `yarn ios` command under the React Native project directory. You will see that the build was successful and that the app is running on the iOS simulator, as follows:

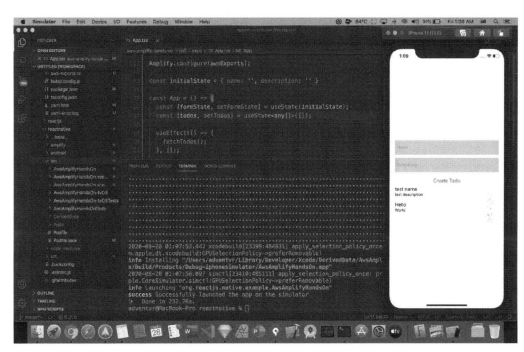

Figure 2.15 – The React Native to-do app running on the iOS simulator

If you run into the Xcode Error: Multiple commands produce error and fail to build the app with React Native due to a specific version being required, which is very common, you will need open the workspace under the ios folder with Xcode, as follows:

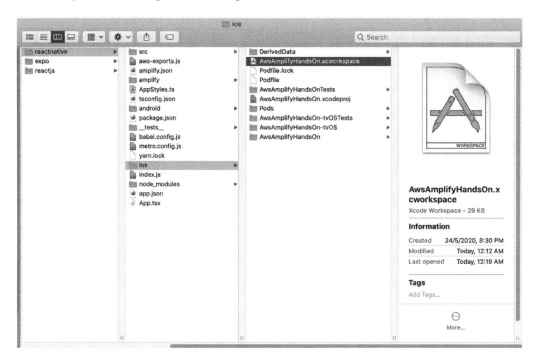

Figure 2.16 – Opening the Xcode workspace

You will see the `Multiple commands produce` errors that are failing the build, as follows:

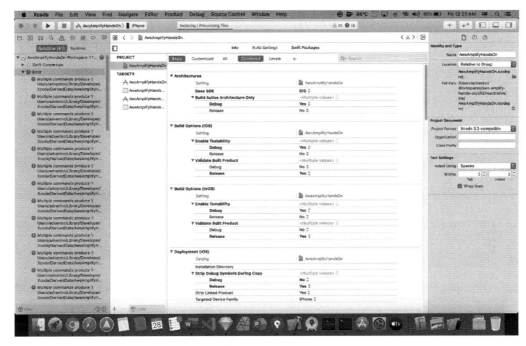

Figure 2.17 – The build failed due to errors

Follow these steps to fix this issue:

1. Select the **AwsAmplifyHandsOn** project from the left menu.

2. Select the **AwsAmplifyHandsOn** project from the middle menu.

3. Select **Build Phases**, open the **Copy Bundle Resources** drop-down list, and remove all the font errors that Xcode is complaining about by pressing the minus (-) button. Make sure that you leave the two important elements there, called `images.xcassets` and `LaunchScreen.xib`, as follows:

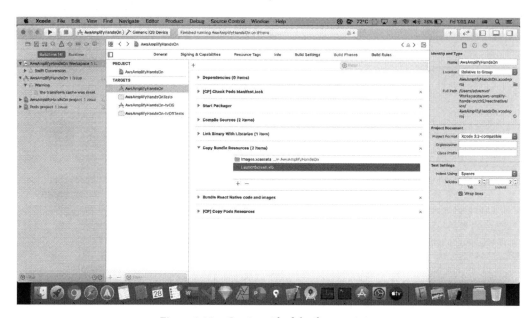

Figure 2.18 – Getting rid of the font settings

Now, let's test the React Native app on the Android emulator by running the `yarn android` command in our Terminal, under the React Native project directory. You should be able to see that the app is running on the Android emulator successfully, as follows:

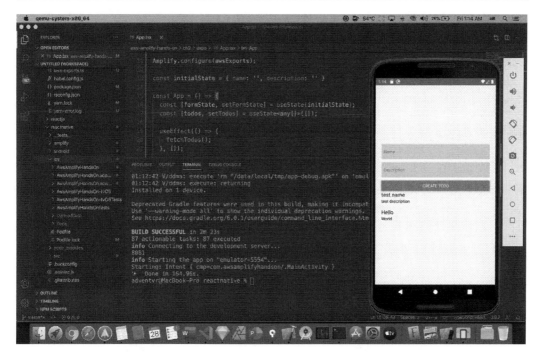

Figure 2.19 – The React Native to-do app running on the Android emulator

As you can see, the benefit of using Expo compared to pure React Native is that it supports web browsers as a platform too. If you have a small team and want to develop a web app as well as a mobile app with a single code base, but without the need to write native code for iOS and Android, then Expo would be the best option for you.

Summary

We finally have our to-do app running on all React frameworks and devices. In this chapter, you learned how to build and run a working to-do list app with ReactJS, Expo, and React Native with AWS Amplify. This means you have enough knowledge to start building apps by yourself. In the next chapter, we will learn how to use pre-built Amplify UI components to speed up our next project.

Section 2: Building a Photo Sharing App

In this section, you will learn how to build a photo sharing app from scratch in a very short amount of time using AWS Amplify and its pluggable UI components. You will learn how to easily build a new product very quickly.

In this section, there are the following chapters:

- *Chapter 3, Pluggable Amplify UI Components*
- *Chapter 4, User Management with Amplify Authentication*
- *Chapter 5, Creating a Blog Post with Amplify GraphQL*
- *Chapter 6, Uploading and Sharing Photos with Amplify Storage*

3
Pluggable Amplify UI Components

Welcome to *Chapter 3, Pluggable Amplify Components*. In this chapter, we will be covering the pre-built and pluggable Amplify UI components. We all know that writing an app or website from scratch can be very time-consuming. Amplify UI components such as sign-up screens, photo albums, and photo pickers are things that can be plug-and-play so that we can test our ideas first and then apply the styles and typography that we want. We will cover the following topics:

- Adding Amplify UI components to the project
- Customizing Amplify UI components
- Applying styling such as typography and colors

We will cover these points for a ReactJS project, an Expo project, and a React Native project.

Technical requirements

This chapter requires you to complete the exercises of *Chapter 1, Getting Familiar with the Amplify CLI and Amplify Console and Chapter 2, Creating a React App with AmplifyJS and TypeScript* in order to add Amplify UI components to your project. You can download the file required from the following link: `https://github.com/PacktPublishing/Rapid-Application-Development-with-AWS-Amplify/tree/master/ch3`.

Installing Amplify UI in the project

Let's go to the project directory of the React app and add the Amplify UI dependencies to the project if you haven't done so.

For a ReactJS project, run the following command in the terminal:

```
yarn add aws-amplify @aws-amplify/ui-react
```

For an Expo or React Native project, run the following command in the terminal:

```
yarn add aws-amplify aws-amplify-react-native
```

The next step is to go to the specific project directory and call the `amplify add auth` command in the terminal in order to set up Amplify UI authentication. We will use an email address as the username in this exercise:

```
amplify add auth
Using service: Cognito, provided by: awscloudformation
 The current configured provider is Amazon Cognito.
 Do you want to use the default authentication and security
 configuration? Default configuration
 Warning: you will not be able to edit these selections.
 How do you want users to be able to sign in? Email
 Do you want to configure advanced settings? No, I am done.
Successfully added resource xxxxxx locally
Some next steps:
"amplify push" will build all your local backend resources and
provision it in the cloud
"amplify publish" will build all your local backend and
frontend resources (if you have hosting category added) and
provision it in the cloud
```

Then, we call the `amplify push` command to provision the authentication backend to the cloud:

```
amplify push
✓ Successfully pulled backend environment dev from the
    cloud.
Current Environment: dev
| Category | Resource name  | Operation | Provider plugin  |
| -------- | -------------- | --------- | ---------------- |
| Auth     | expo1ec0e936   | Create    | awscloudformation |
| Api      | expo           | No Change | awscloudformation |
? Are you sure you want to continue? Yes
∵ Updating resources in the cloud. This may take a few
minutes...
✓ All resources are updated in the cloud
```

Now we are ready to add the Amplify authentication-related UI components to our projects. In the next section, we will be adding different pre-built AWS UI components to the app, such as the authenticator for the user to sign up, sign in, and sign out. We will also show you how to apply theming and customize your components.

Adding Amplify UI components to a ReactJS project

Let's open the `App.tsx` file of our ReactJS project. We will add the following TypeScript code to the app:

1. As usual, import the essential React and Amplify libraries as well as the `App.css` file:

    ```
    import React from 'react';
    import './App.css';
    import Amplify from 'aws-amplify';
    ```

2. Import the `AmplifyAuthenticator` and `AmplifySignOut` UI components. We will integrate the sign in, sign up, and sign out UI components first:

```
import { AmplifyAuthenticator, AmplifySignOut } from '@
aws-amplify/ui-react';
```
```
import { AuthState, onAuthUIStateChange } from '@
aws-amplify/ui-components';
```

3. Import the AWS setting file. Please make sure that you don't commit the `aws-export.js` or `.ts` setting files to the Git repository because the AWS console will figure it out itself:

```
import awsExports from "./aws-exports";
```
```
Amplify.configure(awsExports);
```
```
const App = () => {
```

4. We will create the `authState` and `user` objects with the `useState` hook to keep track of the state of the authentication status of the user. By checking these objects, we can see whether the user is signed in so that we can decide what kind of content to show to the user:

```
const [authState, setAuthState] =
```
```
React.useState<AuthState>();
```
```
const [user, setUser] = React.useState<any |
```
```
undefined>();
```

5. We will use the `useEffect` hook to listen to any changes of the DOM and call the `onAuthUIStateChange` method to set the authentication state and set the user with the authentication data:

```
React.useEffect(() => {
```
```
  return onAuthUIStateChange((nextAuthState,
```
```
  authData) => {
```
```
    setAuthState(nextAuthState);
```
```
    setUser(authData)
```
```
  });
```
```
}, []);
```

6. Now, let's check whether `authState` indicates that the user is logged in and make sure the user data has been retrieved. If the user is logged in, then we will show the welcome screen to the user as well as the sign-out button; if not, then we will show them the sign-in screen, which includes sign-up and reset password screens:

```
return authState === AuthState.SignedIn && user ?
  (
    <div className="container">
      <h2>Amplify UI</h2>
      <h3>Gooday, {user ? user.username :
      'mate'}</h3>
      <p><AmplifySignOut /></p>
    </div>
  ) : (
    <div className="container">
      <AmplifyAuthenticator />
    </div>


  );
}

export default App
```

7. Now let's call the `yarn start` command in the terminal to run the app on the browser; you will see the following sign-in screen:

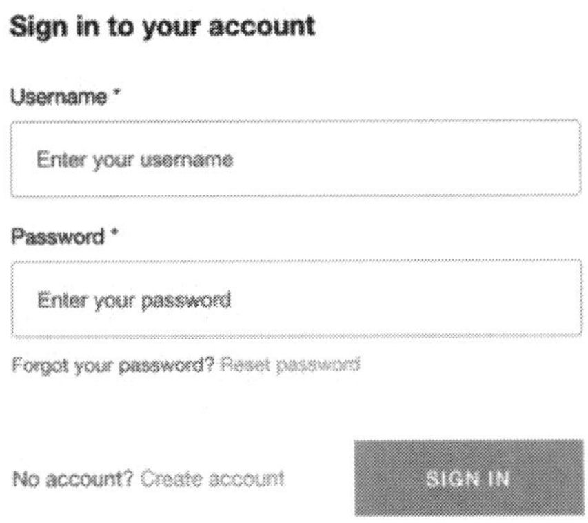

Sign in to your account

Username *

Enter your username

Password *

Enter your password

Forgot your password? Reset password

No account? Create account   SIGN IN

Figure 3.1 – Amplify UI Authenticator component – sign-in screen

When you click on **Create account** on the web page, you will see the sign-up screen:

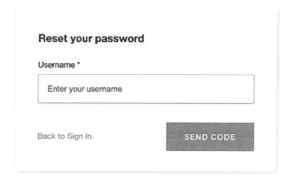

Create a new account

Username *

Username

Password *

Password

Email Address *

Email

Phone Number *

+1 ▼   (555) 555-1212

Have an account? Sign in   CREATE ACCOUNT

Figure 3.2 – Amplify UI Authenticator component – sign-up screen

If you click on **Reset password** on the web page, you will see the reset password screen, where you can click on the **Back to Sign In** button to go back to the sign-in screen:

Reset your password

Username *

Enter your username

Back to Sign In   SEND CODE

Figure 3.3 – Amplify UI Authenticator component – reset password screen

As you can see, the Amplify UI Authenticator component gives you a complete authentication solution out of the box. Imagine if you needed to build all that from scratch, which could take some time to get right.

Let's check out the Image Picker Amplify UI component, which allows users to upload photos to the S3 service:

1. Let's open the `App.tsx` file and import `AmplifyS3ImagePicker` to our code and try it out:

```
import { AmplifyS3ImagePicker } from '@aws-amplify/
ui-react';
```

2. Replace the `AmplifyAuthenticator` tag with the `AmplifyS3ImagePicker` tag to check out the Image Picker component:

```
<div className="container">
    <AmplifyS3ImagePicker />
</div>
```

3. Save the file and the app should be refreshed on the browser, as follows:

Figure 3.4 – Amplify UI Image Picker component

The next step is to customize the authenticator with our own desired wording of what we want to tell the user to do, which we will do in the next section.

Customizing Amplify UI components for ReactJS

Let's open App.tsx, add the AmplifyAuthenticator tag back, start our customization, and import the rest of the authentication components:

1. Import the AmplifySignup, AmplifySignIn, AmplifySignout, and AmplifyForgotPassword components for customization:

    ```
    import { AmplifyAuthenticator, AmplifySignUp,
    AmplifySignIn, AmplifySignOut, AmplifyForgotPassword }
    from '@aws-amplify/ui-react';
    ```

2. The next step is to add the following code blocks inside the AmplifyAuthenticator component. We change the usernameAlias attribute to either username, email, or phone_number. We will use email in our example:

    ```
    <AmplifyAuthenticator usernameAlias="email">
    ```

3. Add the AmplifySignIn code block here and change the values of the attributes, such as headerText and submitButtonText, as appropriate, as well as changing the formFields elements:

    ```
    <AmplifySignIn
            slot="sign-in"
            usernameAlias="email"
            headerText="Please login"
            submitButtonText="Log in"
            formFields={[
                {
                    type: "email",
                    label: "Please enter your email
                    address",
                    placeholder: "you@domain.com",
                    required: true,
                },
                {
                    type: "password",
                    label: "Please enter your password",
                    placeholder: "********",
    ```

```
            required: true,
          }
        ]}
      />
```

4. We will do the same for the `AmplifySignUp` component. Remember to configure the `required` parameters accordingly; that is, if an email address is required for the sign-in form, we should also set `required` to `true` for the sign-up form:

```
<AmplifySignUp
    slot="sign-up"
    usernameAlias="email"
    headerText="Please sign up here:"
    haveAccountText="Already have an
account?"
    submitButtonText="Sign up"
    formFields={[
      {
        type: "email",
        label: "Please enter your email",
        placeholder: "you@domain.com",
        required: true,
      },
      {
        type: "password",
        label: "Please use a strong
password",
        placeholder: "********",
        required: true,
      },
      {
        type: "phone_number",
        label: "Please enter your phone
number",
        placeholder: "123-123-1234",
        required: false,
      },
```

```
              ]}
          />
```

5. For the `AmplifyForgotPassword` tag, we could try the simpler way, which closes the `AmplifyForgotPassword` tag within the opening tag with `/>`:

```
<AmplifyForgotPassword
    slot="forgot-password"
    usernameAlias="email"
    headerText="Forgot Password" />
</AmplifyAuthenticator>
```

Once we have written the code to the `App.tsx` file and saved the new changes, the app should be reloaded automatically on the browser. Let's check out how it looks after we have customized the authentication components. The login screen will change the wording used to whatever we set, which means we can change the language of the text too:

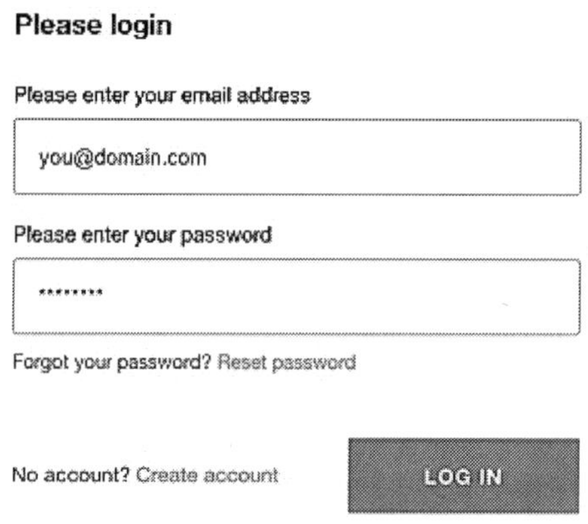

Please login

Please enter your email address

> you@domain.com

Please enter your password

> ....

Forgot your password? Reset password

No account? Create account   **LOG IN**

Figure 3.5 – Customized AmplifySignIn component

The sign-up screen is now changed for using an email address as the username, which could be ideal if your website doesn't require the user to come up with a username:

Please sign up here:

Please enter your email

you@domain.com

Plase use a strong password

****

Plase enter your phone number

+1 ▼   123-123-1234

Already have an account? Sign in   SIGN UP

Figure 3.6 – Customized AmplifySignUp component

Now check out the forgotten password component, whose container doesn't look very consistent with the previous component in terms of proportions. We will cover how to style the container and each element in the next section:

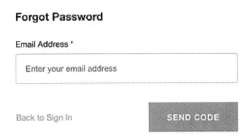

Forgot Password

Email Address *

Enter your email address

Back to Sign In   SEND CODE

Figure 3.7 – Customized AmplifyForgotPassword component

So, the customization of the authentication UI components is almost done. We still want to do some work in terms of styling and typography to keep it consistent with the rest of the website and branding. So, let's jump right into the next section.

Applying styling such as typography and colors to a ReactJS app

Every website, app, or company has its own branding strategy to differentiate itself from others. In this section, we will pick a typography style that is suitable for our project and then change the colors and styling accordingly:

1. Pick a font that you like from `https://fonts.google.com`, and then we will use it as the font of our project:

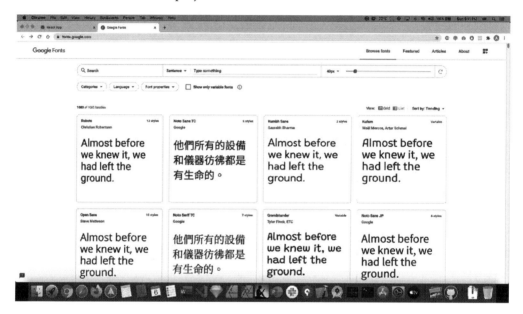

Figure 3.8 – Google Fonts

As you can see, we have over 1,000 options here to choose from; let's pick something that you like and write down the name of it.

2. In this example, we picked something that sounds cool – *Great Vibes* – but is not really readable for the users as an experiment to see how it looks with our app:

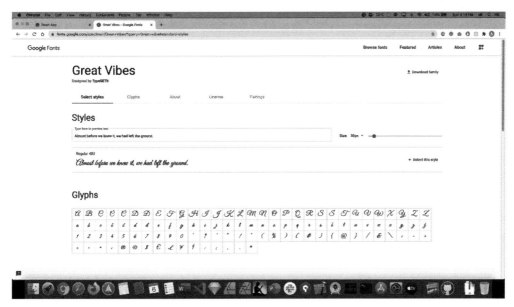

Figure 3.9 – Google Fonts – Great Vibes

3. Now open the App.css file and enter the following code block at the top of the file:

```
@import url('https://fonts.googleapis.com/
css2?family=Great+Vibes');
```

4. The CSS now imports the font called Great Vibes from the Google Fonts
    website, and we set 1em as the base font size for all fonts. Now add the following
    CSS code to the bottom of the App.css file, which will override amplify-font-
    family with Great Vibes:

```
amplify-authenticator {
    --amplify-font-family: 'Great Vibes', serif
    !important;
}
```

5. Now brace yourself and check out how it looks with `Great Vibes`:

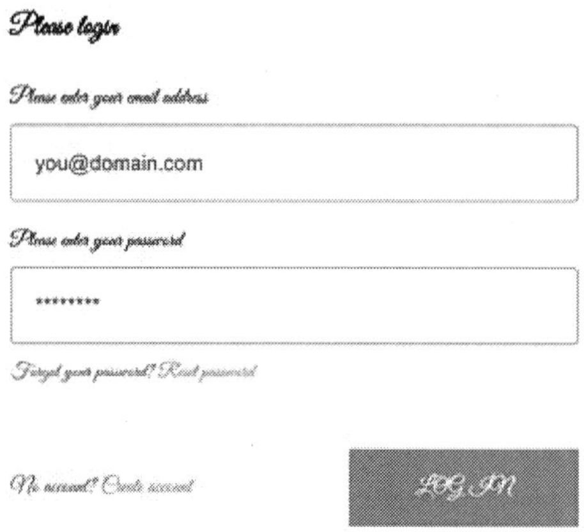

Figure 3.10 – Great Vibes applied

Okay, you get the idea of how to pick a font now – of course, `Great Vibes` is not really readable, but I wanted to show you the differences between before and after so you will know how it works. Now it's your chance to try something better. If you can't think of anything, try `Oswald`, which might look a bit more readable.

As we mentioned earlier, the overall styling might not match the vibe of your website, such as the size of the container and the color of the buttons.

Let's add our desired colors. If you like blue, you can change it to blue; in our case, we picked red to see the effect:

```
:root{
  --amplify-primary-color: red;
  --amplify-primary-tint: red;
  --amplify-primary-shade: red;
}
```

Save the `App.css` file and then go to the browser and check out the new changes:

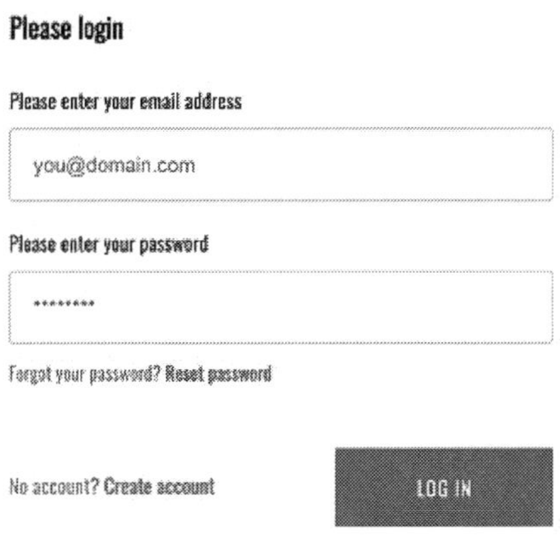

Figure 3.11 – Applying red and the Oswald font

Alright, let's get rid of the drop shadow and the border next, because the container size keeps changing between screens, which can be a look-and-feel problem for many websites. Add the following lines at the bottom of the App.css file:

```
amplify-authenticator {
    --background-color: none;
    --box-shadow: none;
}
```

It looks much better without the border and the drop shadows. When we change between the sign-in and forgotten password screens, we won't see the container changing its size anymore:

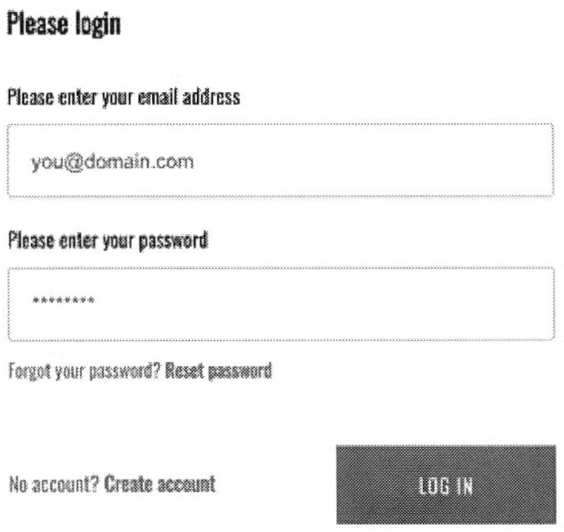

Figure 3.12 – Customizing the UI component CSS – getting rid of the border and drop shadows

Let me give you some references for what you can change in terms of *theming* next, because they're hard to find for those who are not familiar with AWS Amplify:

1. This is the original *Customizing CSS* of the `AmplifyAuthenticator` component styling, which you can change accordingly for your project:

```
amplify-authenticator {
    --background-color: var(--amplify-background-
    color);
    --width: 28.75rem;
    --min-width: 20rem;
    -webkit-font-smoothing: antialiased;
    --box-shadow: 1px 1px 4px 0 rgba(0, 0, 0, 0.15);
    --border-radius: 6px;
    --padding: 35px 40px;
    --margin-bottom: 20px;
    display: flex;
    justify-content: center;
    align-items: center;
    flex: 1;
    height: 100vh;
}
```

2. This is the original *Theming CSS* of the typography styling and colors for Amplify UI components, which you can adjust accordingly for your project:

```
:root {
    --amplify-font-family: 'Amazon Ember', 'Helvetica
    Neue', 'Helvetica', 'Arial', sans-serif;
    --amplify-text-xxs: 0.75rem;
    --amplify-text-xs: 0.81rem;
    --amplify-text-sm: 0.875rem;
    --amplify-text-md: 1rem;
    --amplify-text-md-sub: 1.15rem;
    --amplify-text-lg: 1.5rem;
    --amplify-text-xl: 2rem;
    --amplify-text-xxl: 2.5rem;
    --amplify-primary-color: #ff9900;
```

```
    --amplify-primary-contrast: var(--amplify-white);
    --amplify-primary-tint: #ffac31;
    --amplify-primary-shade: #e88b01;
    --amplify-secondary-color: #152939;
    --amplify-secondary-contrast: var(--amplify-
white);
    --amplify-secondary-tint: #31465f;
    --amplify-secondary-shade: #1F2A37;
    --amplify-tertiary-color: #5d8aff;
    --amplify-tertiary-contrast: var(--amplify-white);
    --amplify-tertiary-tint: #7da1ff;
    --amplify-tertiary-shade: #537BE5;
    --amplify-background-color: var(--amplify-white);
    --amplify-grey: #828282;
    --amplify-light-grey: #c4c4c4;
    --amplify-white: #ffffff;
    --amplify-smoke-white: #f5f5f5;
    --amplify-red: #dd3f5b;
    --amplify-blue: #099ac8;
}
```

In the next section, we will go through the styling steps for the React Native and Expo apps. Since the React Native and Expo apps don't support CSS, we will use React styling instead.

Adding Amplify UI components to a React Native project

In this section, we will cover the steps of how to implement Amplify UI components for a React Native app. Before we do that, we need to make sure we have installed the dependencies by entering the following command in the terminal:

```
yarn add aws-amplify aws-amplify-react-native
```

Once we have added the Amplify libraries to the Expo or React Native project, we would like to test the Authenticator UI library. There are two ways to do that: using the `withAuthenticator` **Higher-Order Component** (**HOC**) or using the actual `Authenticator` component. We picked the `withAuthenticator` component as an example. Let's add the following code to the existing `App.tsx` file:

```
import React from 'react';
import { withAuthenticator } from 'aws-amplify-react-native';
import Amplify from 'aws-amplify';

import awsExports from "./aws-exports";
Amplify.configure(awsExports);

const App = () => {
  return (
    ...
  )
}
export default withAuthenticator(App);
```

But you will see there is a type error because the Amplify React Native library does not support TypeScript yet:

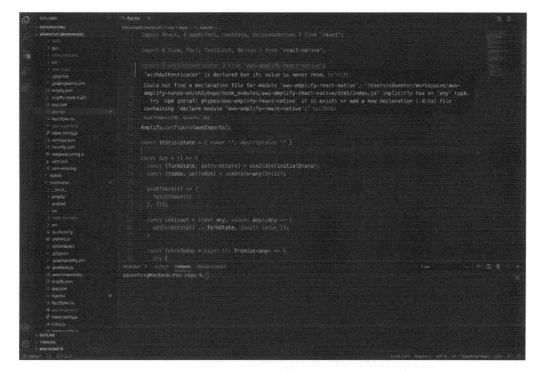

Figure 3.13 – Type error of the Amplify React Native UI library

Let's create a react-app-env.d.ts file under the src folder of the project directory with the following code:

```
declare module "aws-amplify-react-native";
```

The type error should now be gone from the code editor seen in *Figure 3.6*. We can now run the `yarn ios` command to test the Amplify Authenticator UI component for the Expo and React Native apps:

1. The Expo app is running successfully on the iOS simulator:

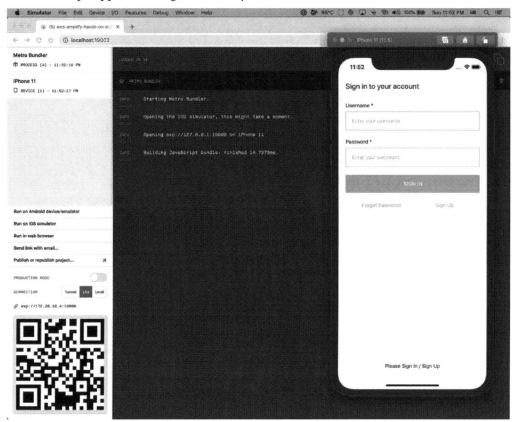

Figure 3.14 – The Expo app is running successfully with the Amplify Authenticator UI component

2. The React Native app is running successfully on the iOS simulator:

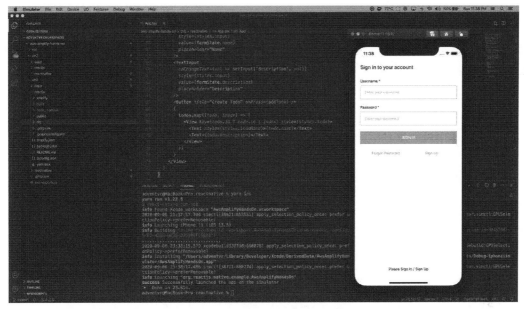

Figure 3.15 – The React Native app is running successfully with
the Amplify Authenticator UI component

With little effort, AWS Amplify really helps us to save a lot of development time, especially when developing apps, because UI components take time to make. In the next section, we will focus on customization and theming, just as we did with the ReactJS project.

Customizing Amplify UI components for Expo and React Native apps

AWS Amplify for React Native is a little bit less customizable compared to Amplify for ReactJS – perhaps that's because it is still new. We can only customize the sign-up screen, instead of all the screens as we did with the ReactJS app. But we can still configure what is to be used as the username, choosing between `username`, `email`, and `phone_number`. Let's open `App.tsx` and do the following:

1. Import the `react` and `react-native` libraries:

```
import React from 'react';
import { Text } from 'react-native';
```

2.   Import the `withAuthenticator` component from the `aws-amplify-react-native` library. This is an HOC, which is a function that takes a component and returns a new component. In our case, we will use it to wrap around the `App` component and return it with the Amplify Authenticator component:

```
import { withAuthenticator } from 'aws-amplify-react-native';
import Amplify from 'aws-amplify';
import awsExports from "./aws-exports";
Amplify.configure(awsExports);
```

3.   Show something to the user after they have logged in to the app, such as `Hello World` as a welcome message, using the `Text` component:

```
const App = async () => {
  return (
    <Text>Hello world</Text>
  );
};
```

4.   Create a `signUpConfig` object to customize the settings of the sign-up screen, such as the header text, the default country code of the phone number, and so on. We will change the default country code to 852, which is Hong Kong, as an example:

```
const signUpConfig = {
  header: 'Please sign up here',
  hideAllDefaults: true,
  defaultCountryCode: '852',
```

5.   For `signUpFields`, we can change the labels and placeholder text of each field, such as email, password, and phone number. Since the term "phone number" could be a bit misleading if you choose `phone_number` for `usernameAttributes`, you might want to change the label to "mobile number," because the confirmation code will be sent as an SMS to the user's mobile number. Just "phone number" could mean a home phone number or a work phone number that can't receive SMS:

```
  signUpFields: [
    {
      label: 'Please enter your email',
      key: 'email',
```

```
        placeholder: 'abc@domain.com',
        required: true,
        displayOrder: 1,
        type: 'string'
      },
      {
        label: 'Please enter a strong password',
        key: 'password',
        placeholder: '********',
        required: true,
        displayOrder: 2,
        type: 'password'
      },
      {
        label: 'Please enter your mobile number',
        key: 'phone_number',
        placeholder: 'mobile number',
        required: false,
        displayOrder: 3,
        type: 'string'
      }
    ]
};
```

6. We use `withAuthenticator` to wrap around the `App` component in order for the authenticator to be generated for the app. We will set `usernameAttributes` to `email` and set `signUpConfig` to the `signUpConfig` object:

```
export default withAuthenticator(App,
  {
    usernameAttributes: 'email',
    signUpConfig: signUpConfig
  });
```

Alright, let's test the new changes on both the iOS Simulator and the Android Emulator to see how they look:

1. Enter the yarn ios command in the terminal to launch the Expo app on the iOS simulator or yarn android for the Android Emulator.

2. Click **SIGN UP** on the screen to see the new changes to the sign-up screen:

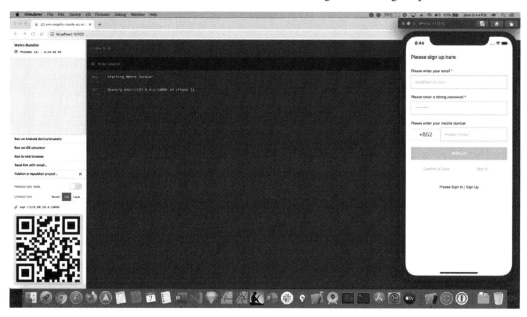

Figure 3.16 – The sign-up screen on iOS

3. Now click the **Run on Android device/emulator** button on the browser to check out the Expo app on Android:

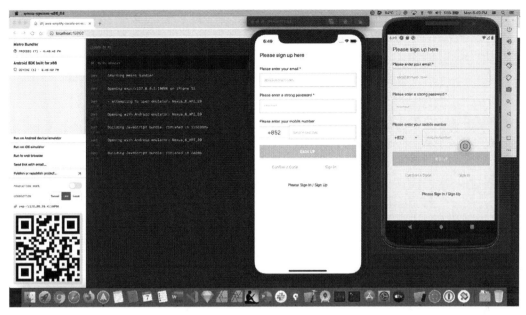

Figure 3.17 – The sign-up screen on Android alongside the iOS version

We have done all we can to customize the Amplify Authenticator UI component so far. The code for Expo and React Native is the same, so we don't need to worry about any differences between the two. In the next section, we will show you how to change the theme of your app.

Applying styling such as typography and colors to Expo and React Native apps

Theming on React Native and Expo is slightly different from ReactJS because there is only one way to do it, which is by creating a style file that contains all the styles instead of a CSS file. Let's create a file called AmplifyUIStyles.ts in the app directory and do the following:

1. Import StyleSheet from the react-native module:

    ```
    import { StyleSheet } from 'react-native';
    ```

2. Export the `AmplifyThemeType` type and the colors. You can change the colors to whatever you want with a hex color, or you can just use the name of a color, as here with `'blue'`:

```
export type AmplifyThemeType = Record<string, any>;
// Colors
export const deepSquidInk = '#152939';
export const linkUnderlayColor = '#FFF';
export const errorIconColor = '#DD3F5B';
export const textInputColor = '#000000';
export const textInputBorderColor = '#C4C4C4';
export const placeholderColor = '#C7C7CD';
export const buttonColor = 'blue';
export const disabledButtonColor = 'blue';
```

3. The next step is to change the styling of the container and each section as you like:

```
// Theme
export default StyleSheet.create({
    container: {
        flex: 1,
        flexDirection: 'column',
        alignItems: 'center',
        justifyContent: 'space-around',
        paddingTop: 20,
        width: '100%',
        backgroundColor: '#FFF',
    },
    section: {
        flex: 1,
        width: '100%',
        justifyContent: 'space-between',
        paddingHorizontal: 20,
    },
    sectionScroll: {
        flex: 1,
        width: '100%',
        paddingHorizontal: 20,
```

```
    },
    sectionHeader: {
        width: '100%',
        marginBottom: 32,
        paddingTop: 20,
    },
```

4. For the header, we will show you how to apply typography by adding a `fontFamily` attribute with the value of the font; we chose `HelveticaNeue-CondensedBold` as an example:

```
    sectionHeaderText: {
        color: deepSquidInk,
        fontSize: 20,
        fontWeight: '500',
        fontFamily: 'HelveticaNeue-CondensedBold'
    },
    sectionFooter: {
        width: '100%',
        padding: 10,
        flexDirection: 'row',
        justifyContent: 'space-between',
        marginTop: 15,
        marginBottom: 20,
    },
```

5. We can also change the font size for the footer text to something a bit bigger, such as `16`:

```
    sectionFooterLink: {
        fontSize: 16,
        color: buttonColor,
        alignItems: 'baseline',
        textAlign: 'center',
    },
    sectionFooterLinkDisabled: {
        fontSize: 16,
        color: disabledButtonColor,
```

```
        alignItems: 'baseline',
        textAlign: 'center',
    },
```

6. For the navbar, we will change `marginTop` to `50` and set `alignItems` to `center` to see how it looks; feel free to change the value to something else. The value is aligned with the CSS standard:

```
    navBar: {
        marginTop: 50,
        padding: 15,
        flexDirection: 'row',
        justifyContent: 'flex-end',
        alignItems: 'center',
    },
    navButton: {
        marginLeft: 12,
        borderRadius: 4,
    },
    cell: {
        flex: 1,
        width: '50%',
    },
```

7. For `errorRow`, we will change `justifyContent` to `center`:

```
    errorRow: {
        flexDirection: 'row',
        justifyContent: 'center',
    },
    errorRowText: {
        marginLeft: 10,
    },
    photo: {
        width: '100%',
    },
    album: {
        width: '100%',
```

```
    },
    button: {
        backgroundColor: buttonColor,
        alignItems: 'center',
        padding: 16,
    },
    buttonDisabled: {
        backgroundColor: disabledButtonColor,
        alignItems: 'center',
        padding: 16,
    },
```

8. For buttonText, I want it to look a bit bigger, so I'll change it to 16:

```
    buttonText: {
        color: '#fff',
        fontSize: 16,
        fontWeight: '600',
    },
    formField: {
        marginBottom: 22,
    },
    input: {
        padding: 16,
        borderWidth: 1,
        borderRadius: 3,
        borderColor: textInputBorderColor,
        color: textInputColor,
    },
    inputLabel: {
        marginBottom: 8,
    },
    phoneContainer: {
        display: 'flex',
        flexDirection: 'row',
        alignItems: 'center',
    },
```

9. For `phoneInput`, I want to give it a bit more padding, so I'll change the padding to `20`:

```
    phoneInput: {
        flex: 2,
        padding: 20,
        borderWidth: 1,
        borderRadius: 3,
        borderColor: textInputBorderColor,
        color: textInputColor,
    },
    picker: {
        flex: 1,
        height: 44,
    },
    pickerItem: {
        height: 44,
    },
    signedOutMessage: {
        textAlign: 'center',
        padding: 20,
    },
});
```

10. Let's import the newly created `AmplifyUIStyles` file into our main app, which is the `App.tsx` file, as follows:

```
import React from 'react';
import { Text } from 'react-native';
import { withAuthenticator } from 'aws-amplify-react-native';
import Amplify from 'aws-amplify';
```

11. Import the new style as a theme with an easy-to-remember name; I called
    it GreatTheme here:

```
import GreatTheme from './AmplifyUIStyles';
import awsExports from "./aws-exports";
Amplify.configure(awsExports);


const App = async () => {
  return (
    <Text>Hello world</Text>
  );
};


const signUpConfig = {
  ...
};
```

12. Add GreatTheme to the last slot of the withAuthenticator input parameters:

```
export default withAuthenticator(App,
  {
    usernameAttributes: 'email',
    signUpConfig: signUpConfig
  }, [], null, GreatTheme
)
```

13. Now let's run `yarn ios` again to check out the new changes to the app. This time, we will use the exact same code from the Expo app on the React Native app to show you that code can be shared between two projects:

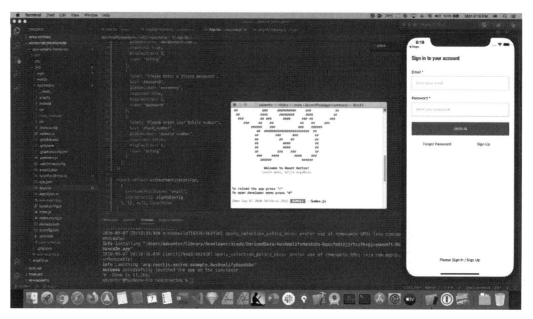

Figure 3.18 – The color has changed as well as the font of the header on iOS

14. For Android, we will change `frontFamily` to `Roboto` and then run the `yarn android` command in the terminal to see the new changes on the Android Emulator:

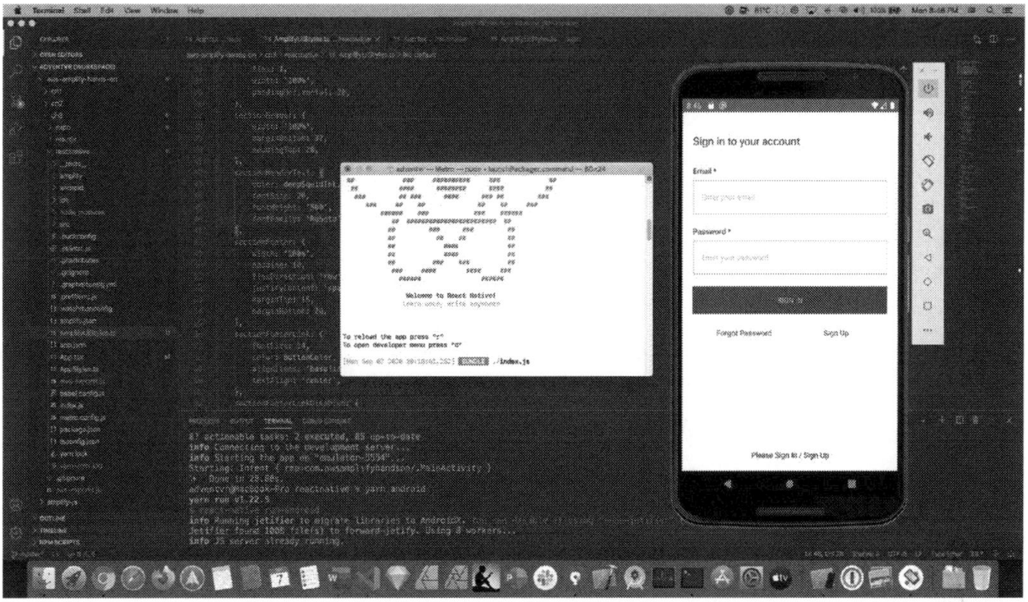

Figure 3.19 – The color has changed as well as the font of the header on Android

We have covered how to customize and theme Amplify UI components for both React Native and Expo apps in this section. If you want to do further customization, you can try to change the background color or add a background image as an exercise.

Summary

In this chapter, we learned how to add Amplify UI components to our projects and about customizing and theming the Amplify UI Authentication component. It really is that easy to add authentication to your app, with just a few lines of code. The AWS Amplify UI components really give us a head start in terms of the development speed; we can save a lot of man-hours in perfecting the sign-up and login flow. Since we have now added an authentication component to our app, in the next chapter, we will be going through how to implement user management with the Amplify authentication backend, which is AWS Cognito.

4
User Management with Amplify Authentication

In this chapter, we will continue from where we left off in the previous chapter; that is, integrating the Amplify authentication UI with the Amplify authentication backend. Setting up the user management system correctly is critical for many businesses and websites because the security surrounding user information is very important. In this chapter, we will cover the following topics:

- Understanding AWS authentication
- Signing up for the ReactJS app
- Signing in and out of the ReactJS app
- Signing up for the Expo and React Native apps
- Signing in and out of the Expo and React Native apps

We will cover these points for a ReactJS project, an Expo project, and a React Native project.

Technical requirements

This chapter requires that you have completed the exercises in the past three chapters, so that you can add the Amplify UI component to your project. Make sure that you have installed and configured the Amplify CLI as well. You can download the necessary file from the following link: `https://github.com/PacktPublishing/Rapid-Application-Development-with-AWS-Amplify/tree/master/ch4`.

> **Important Note**
>
> If you want to reuse the same cloud backend with different folders for each chapter with the code you've downloaded from the public repository, place the working `aws-exports.js` or `.ts` file in the project folder, and then simply call the `amplify init` and `amplify pull` commands to initialize and pull the resources to the specific chapter project folder.

Understanding AWS authentication

The AWS Amplify Framework uses **Amazon Cognito** as its provider for authentication. Amazon Cognito is a robust user management suite that includes all the latest identity and access management standards, such as **OAuth 2.0**, **SAML 2.0**, and **OpenID Connect**.

Since it's a SaaS solution, you will have a free tier of 50,000 **Monthly Active Users** (**MAUs**) to start your next project, until you hit the limit and start paying the paid tier of each additional user that is above the free tier. It can be scaled to millions of users without you trying to figure out a solution to tackle the scalability problem. This is because it is all being handled behind the scenes, which takes all the stress away from all the scalability issues that you might be facing for your potentially super successful product.

In this tutorial, you'll learn how to add authentication to your application using Amazon Cognito and how to log in with a username with password. We will add authentication to the Amplify backend. This way, you can remove and re-add it if you want to change the selection. Let's get started:

1. Call the `amplify add auth` command for the Amplify project, if you haven't done so already:

```
amplify add auth
Using service: Cognito, provided by: awscloudformation
 The current configured provider is Amazon Cognito.
 Do you want to use the default authentication and
 security configuration? Default configuration
```

```
Warning: you will not be able to edit these selections.

How do you want users to be able to sign in? Email

Do you want to configure advanced settings? No, I am
done.

Successfully added resource xxxxx locally

Some next steps:

"amplify push" will build all your local backend
resources and provision it in the cloud

"amplify publish" will build all your local backend and
frontend resources (if you have hosting category added)
and provision it in the cloud
```

As indicated by Warning: you will not be able to edit these selections, if you really want to change some of the settings, you can call the amplify remove auth command to remove the authentication backend and add it back. If you have a running app in production, make sure you have the backup data for your user pool before calling the remove command. This is because it will remove everything that is not reversable. So, make sure you only call the remove command during development.

2. Now, call the amplify push command to push the new changes to the cloud:

```
amplify push
✔ Successfully pulled backend environment dev from the
cloud.

Current Environment: dev

| Category | Resource name      | Operation | Provider
plugin   |
| -------- | ------------------ | --------- | -----------
------ |
| Auth     | reactjsappxxxxx    | Create    |
awscloudformation |
| Api      | reactjsapp         | No Change |
awscloudformation |
| Hosting  | amplifyhosting     | No Change |
awscloudformation |
? Are you sure you want to continue? Yes
```

```
⠋ Updating resources in the cloud. This may take a few
minutes...
✓ All resources are updated in the cloud
```

3. This could take a couple of minutes. Now, let's use the `amplify remove auth` command to remove the authentication from the cloud. We're doing this because we want to use a username to sign in instead of an email:

```
amplify remove auth

Scanning for plugins...

Plugin scan successful


You have configured resources that might depend on this
Cognito resource.  Updating this Cognito resource could
have unintended side effects.

? Choose the resource you would want to remove
reactjsappxxxxx

? Are you sure you want to delete the resource? This
action deletes all files related to this resource from
the backend directory. Yes

Successfully removed resource
```

4. Now, let's call the `amplify add auth` command again, but we will choose a username for the user to sign in:

```
amplify add auth

Do you want to use the default authentication and
security configuration? (Use arrow keys)

❯ Default configuration

  Default configuration with Social Provider (Federation)

  Manual configuration

  I want to learn more.

Do you want to use the default authentication and
security configuration? Default configuration

  Warning: you will not be able to edit these selections.

  How do you want users to be able to sign in? (Use arrow
keys)

❯ Username

  Email

  Phone Number
```

```
   Email or Phone Number
    I want to learn more.
How do you want users to be able to sign in? Username
  Do you want to configure advanced settings? (Use arrow
keys)
> No, I am done.
    Yes, I want to make some additional changes.
How do you want users to be able to sign in? Username
  Do you want to configure advanced settings? No, I am
done.
Successfully added auth resource reactjsxxxxxxx locally


Some next steps:
"amplify push" will build all your local backend
resources and provision it in the cloud
"amplify publish" will build all your local backend and
frontend resources (if you have hosting category added)
and provision it in the cloud
```

5. Once we have removed the old authentication backend and added the new
    authentication backend, we must call `amplify push` to push the changes
    to the cloud:

```
amplify push
   ✔ Successfully pulled backend environment dev from the
cloud.
Current Environment: dev
| Category | Resource name      | Operation | Provider
plugin   |
| -------- | ------------------ | --------- | -----------
------ |
| Auth     | reactjsappxxxxxxxa | Create    |
awscloudformation |
| Auth     | reactjsappxxxxxxxb | Delete    |
awscloudformation |
| Api      | reactjsapp         | No Change |
awscloudformation |
| Hosting  | amplifyhosting     | No Change |
awscloudformation |
```

```
? Are you sure you want to continue? Yes
⠿ Updating resources in the cloud. This may take a few
  minutes...
✔ All resources are updated in the cloud
```

6. Once you have pushed the new changes to the cloud, you can configure the Cognito console (`https://console.aws.amazon.com/cognito/users`). Click on the **App clients** option on the left-hand side menu, and then click on both the **Show Details** buttons on the main screen to expand the options for both the app and web clients:

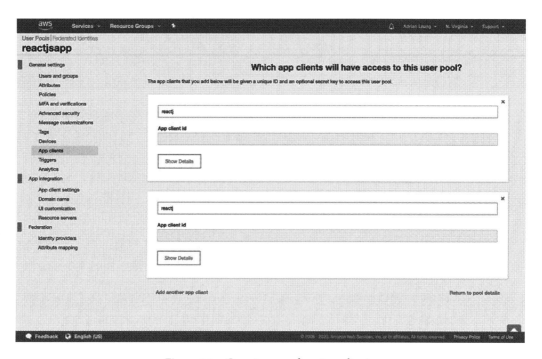

Figure 4.1 – Cognito console – App clients

7. For both the app client and web client sections, check the **Enable username password based authentication (ALLOW_USER_PASSWORD_AUTH)** checkbox; uncheck the rest of the options. Choose the **Enabled (Recommended)** option under the **Prevent Users Existence Errors** section and then hit the **Save app client changes** button for both sections:

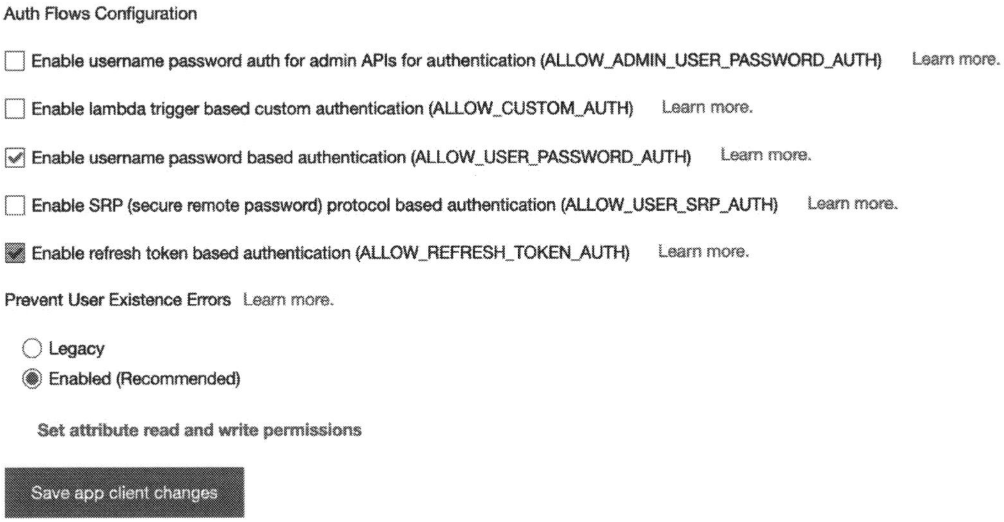

Auth Flows Configuration

☐ Enable username password auth for admin APIs for authentication (ALLOW_ADMIN_USER_PASSWORD_AUTH)   Learn more.

☐ Enable lambda trigger based custom authentication (ALLOW_CUSTOM_AUTH)   Learn more.

☑ Enable username password based authentication (ALLOW_USER_PASSWORD_AUTH)   Learn more.

☐ Enable SRP (secure remote password) protocol based authentication (ALLOW_USER_SRP_AUTH)   Learn more.

☑ Enable refresh token based authentication (ALLOW_REFRESH_TOKEN_AUTH)   Learn more.

Prevent User Existence Errors Learn more.

○ Legacy
◉ Enabled (Recommended)

  Set attribute read and write permissions

```
Save app client changes
```

Figure 4.2 – Cognito console – App clients – Save app client changes

The next step is optional, which is to raise the daily email limit from 1,000 to unlimited (**Pay as You Go (PAYG)**) if you decide to take your app live and let many users use it.

8. Go to the Amazon Cognito console again (`https://console.aws.amazon.com/cognito/users`) and click on **Message customizations** on the left menu bar:

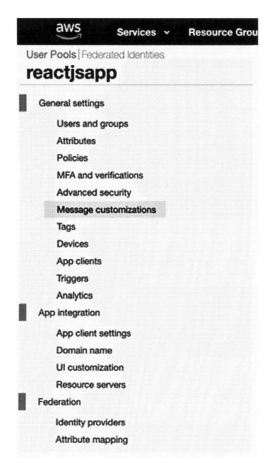

Figure 4.3 – Amazon Cognito console – Message customizations

9. Select **Yes – Use Amazon SES** (**Amazon Simple Email Service**) below **Do you want to send emails through your Amazon SES Configuration?** and fill in the rest of the form, including the **FROM** email address and **REPLY-TO** email address (make sure you click on **Verify an SES identity** to verify the email address first). Then, click **Save changes**:

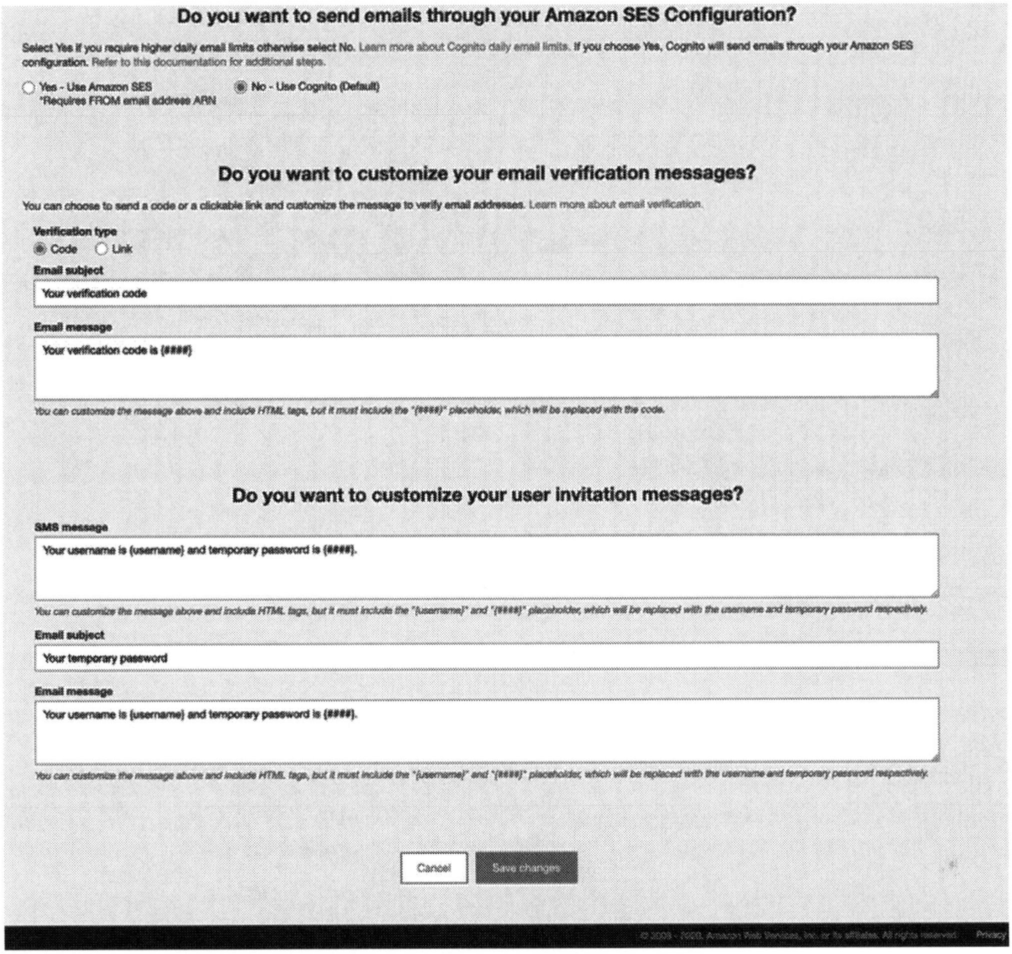

Figure 4.4 – Amazon Cognito console – Amazon SES

Raising the daily email limit is important before the app goes live as you don't want your potential users not being able to receive important emails, such as those containing confirmation codes and reset password instructions.

Now that we are done, we will integrate the app with the new authentication backend.

Signing up for the ReactJS app

In the previous chapter, we created the sign-up and sign-in form with the Amplify UI. Now, we will make a small modification to the original code.

Let's open the App.jsx file and replace the entire original code with the following code. We will use the withAutenticator component this time:

1. Import the withAuthenticator and AmplifySignOut Amplify UI components to keep the code simple and lean. Then, import the Auth Amplify library:

```
import React from 'react';
import './App.css';
import Amplify, { Auth } from 'aws-amplify';
import { AuthState, onAuthUIStateChange } from '@
aws-amplify/ui-components';
import { withAuthenticator, AmplifySignOut } from '@
aws-amplify/ui-react';

import awsExports from "./aws-exports";
Amplify.configure(awsExports);
```

2. Make sure that you configure the authenticationFlowType parameter with the USER_PASSWORD_AUTH value. This tells the Cognito service to use the password authentication flow to avoid any authentication errors:

```
Auth.configure({
   authenticationFlowType: 'USER_PASSWORD_AUTH'
});

const App = () => {
   const [authState, setAuthState] =
   React.useState<AuthState>();
   const [user, setUser] = React.useState<any |
   undefined>();

   React.useEffect(() => {
      return onAuthUIStateChange((nextAuthState, authData)
      => {
         setAuthState(nextAuthState);
         setUser(authData)
      });
   }, []);
```

```
return (
    <div className="container">
```

3. We greet the user with their username if the username exists:

```
        <h3>Good day, {authState === AuthState.SignedIn &&
        user
        ? user.username : 'mate'}</h3>
        <p><AmplifySignOut /></p>
    </div>
    )
}
```

Wrap the entire app with the `withAuthenticator` **High-Order Component** (**HOC**). This is a wrapper component that will return a new component based on the input component, as follows:

```
export default withAuthenticator(App);
```

Once we've saved these new changes, we can call the `yarn start` command in the terminal to test them:

1. Click the **Create account** link to create a new account:

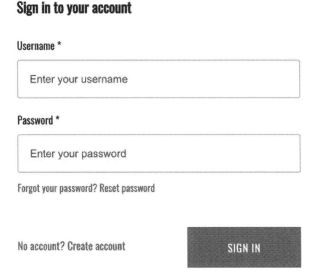

Figure 4.5 – Sign-in screen – Create account

2. Fill in the sign-up form with a unique username, a strong password that contains at least 8 characters, a working email address to receive the confirmation code, and a working mobile number. Then, click **CREATE ACCOUNT**:

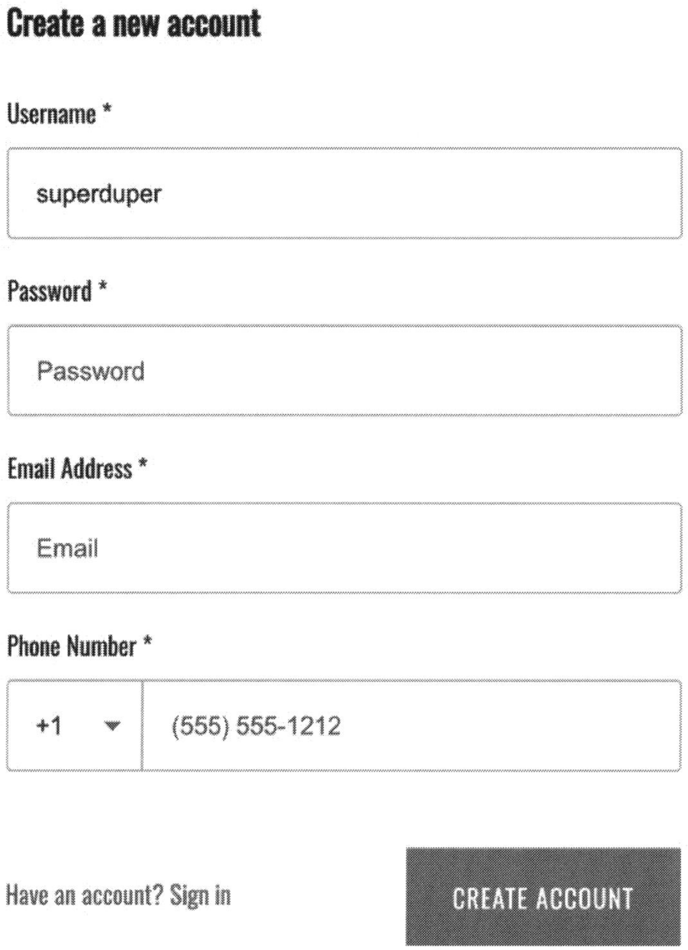

Create a new account

Username *

> superduper

Password *

> Password

Email Address *

> Email

Phone Number *

> +1   ▼   (555) 555-1212

Have an account? Sign in

CREATE ACCOUNT

Figure 4.6 – Create a new account screen

3. You will see the **Confirm Sign up** screen and receive a confirmation email called **Your verification code**. Enter the 6-digit code you receive in the **Confirmation Code** field then click on the **CONFIRM** button:

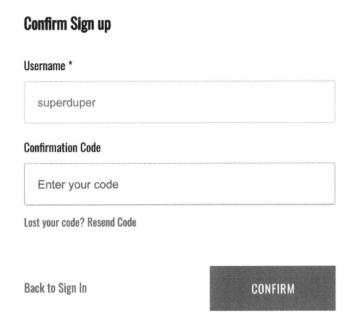

Figure 4.7 – Confirm Sign up screen

4. Once you enter the confirmation code, you will see a greeting message that says **Good day, [username]** and the **SIGN OUT** button. If you click on the **SIGN OUT** button, it will take you back to the sign-in screen:

Figure 4.8 – Confirm Sign up screen

As you can see, the entire app has been protected by the withAuthenticator HOC component, thus enabling authentication and authorization for the entire app. In this case, users must log in before they can use the app. In the next section, we will deploy the app to an environment with a publicly accessible URL that you can share with anyone to try out your app.

Signing in and out of the ReactJS app

We have got the authentication working locally, but does it work when we deploy it to the internet? Let's find out! In this section, we will show you how to deploy the app to an environment with AWS Amplify hosting:

1. If you haven't added hosting to the Amplify project yet, you can call the `amplify add hosting` and `amplify push` commands beforehand. Let's call the `amplify publish` command in the terminal to publish the ReactJS app to the cloud. This will generate a publicly accessible URL:

```
amplify publish
  ✔ Successfully pulled backend environment dev from the cloud.
Current Environment: dev
| Category | Resource name      | Operation | Provider
plugin    |
| -------- | ------------------ | --------- | -----------
------ |
| Api      | reactjsapp         | No Change |
awscloudformation |
| Hosting  | amplifyhosting     | No Change |
awscloudformation |
| Auth     | reactjsappxxxxxxxx | No Change |
awscloudformation |
No changes detected
Publish started for amplifyhosting
...
> react-scripts build
Creating an optimized production build...
Compiled successfully.
File sizes after gzip:
...
  ✔ Zipping artifacts completed.
  ✔ Deployment complete!
https://dev.d3xxxxxx1u.amplifyapp.com
```

2. The Amplify CLI published the build artifacts to the Amplify hosting URL. If you go to the Amplify Console (`https://console.aws.amazon.com/amplify/home`), you will see that the web app has been published successfully:

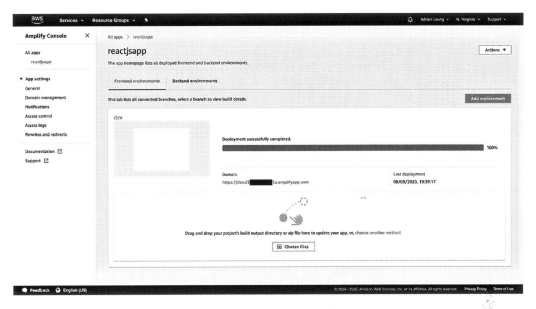

Figure 4.9 – Amplify Console – Amplify hosting

3. Let's grab the URL from the terminal and paste it into the browser. Alternatively, we can click the link on the Amplify Console directly to check out the web app.

4. The web app is running perfectly on the generated URL. We can test it out by entering the username and password for the account that we created previously, and then click the **SIGN IN** button:

Sign in to your account

Username *

superduper

Password *

••••••••

Forgot your password? Reset password

No account? Create account   SIGN IN

Figure 4.10 – Entering the username and password on the sign-in screen

5. Since the login functionality is working perfectly in the cloud, we should be able to see the greeting message and the **SIGN OUT** button, as follows:

Figure 4.11 – Logged in successfully

6. Let's click on the **SIGN OUT** button, which should take us back to the **Sign in to your account** screen:

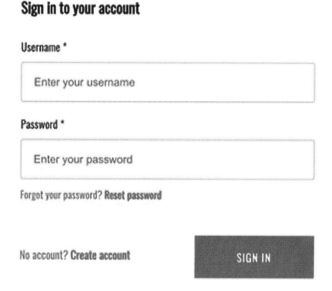

Figure 4.12 – Signed out successfully

With that, we have got authentication working perfectly for the ReactJS app.

In the next section, we will go through similar steps for the Expo and React Native apps. In the meantime, you can try to add more stuff to the app, republish it, and let your friends and family test your new project.

Signing up for the Expo and React Native apps

To be honest, I am very glad that both Expo and React Native can share the same code with the Amplify UI. Because of this, you don't need to worry about if you decided to go with Expo first and want to change it to pure React Native later, since you can reuse the same code base.

We will follow the *Understanding AWS authentication* section of this chapter for the React Native and Expo apps. Here, we must remove the old Cognito user pool, which contains your email as the identifier, and add a new Cognito user pool with the username as the identifier, plus the additional settings, to the Cognito console.

Now, we need to go to the app directory, open the `App.tsx` file, and do the following:

1. Import the necessary libraries, such as the React and the React Native libraries and the Amplify React Native library:

```
import React from 'react';
import { View, Text } from 'react-native';
import { withAuthenticator } from 'aws-amplify-react-
native';
import Amplify, { Auth } from 'aws-amplify';
import awsExports from "./aws-exports";
Amplify.configure(awsExports);
```

2. Configure the Amplify authentication method with the user password flow:

```
Auth.configure({
  authenticationFlowType: 'USER_PASSWORD_AUTH'
});

const App = () => {
  return (
    <View>
      <Text>Hello world</Text>
    </View>
  );
};
export default withAuthenticator(App);
```

3. Call the yarn ios or yarn android command in a terminal to run the app. Try to sign up and then confirm the verification code you received via email. At this point, you will see an **Error: No credentials, applicationId or region** error message, as follows:

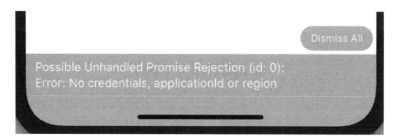

Figure 4.13 – No credentials error

At the time of writing, this is a known issue (https://github.com/aws-amplify/amplify-js/issues/5918) with the Amplify React Native library, and the only way to get rid of the error is to do the following instead:

1. Import the additional style and theme libraries that we will create:

```
import React from 'react';
import { View, Text, Button } from 'react-native';
import styles from './AppStyles';
import { Authenticator } from 'aws-amplify-react-native';
import Amplify, { Auth } from 'aws-amplify';
import GreatTheme from './AmplifyUIStyles';
import awsExports from "./aws-exports";
```

2. Now, we must configure Amplify's settings. First, we will set oauth to an empty object and set the authenticationFlowType parameter to USER_PASSWORD_ AUTH. Then, we must turn Analytics off by setting the disabled parameter to true. This will fix the no credentials error that we mentioned previously:

```
Amplify.configure({
    ...awsExports,
    Auth: {
        oauth: {},
        authenticationFlowType: 'USER_PASSWORD_AUTH'
    },
    Analytics: {
```

```
        disabled: true
    }
  });

const App = () => {
    const [authState, setAuthState] = React
    .useState<any>();
    const [user, setUser] = React.useState<any |
    undefined>();
```

3. Create a `setCurrentUser` method to grab the authenticated user from the `Auth` class:

```
    const setCurrentUser = () => {
      Auth.currentAuthenticatedUser()
        .then((user: any) => {
          setUser(user);
        })
        .catch((info: any) => {
          console.log("Info: ", info);
        });
    };
```

4. If the user exists and is signed in, then we can show the greeting message to the user, along with their username and the **SIGN OUT** button:

```
    return (authState && user) ? (
      <View style={styles.container}>
        <Text>Good day, {(authState && user) ? user.
        username :
        'mate'}</Text>
      </View>
    ) : (
```

5. If the user has not signed in yet, then we can show `Authenticator` instead. The following code will also set the authentication and the user states once the user has logged in:

```
    <Authenticator
        signUpConfig={signUpConfig}
        onStateChange={(authState: any) => {
            setAuthState(authState);
            setCurrentUser();
        }}
        theme={GreatTheme}
    />
    );
};
```

6. Apply the same `signUpConfig` settings that you applied in the previous chapter. We can try to change the country code to something else such as `61`, which is for Australia, if we want to improve the user experience by preselecting the country code for the user:

```
const signUpConfig = {
    header: 'Please sign up here',
    hideAllDefaults: true,
    defaultCountryCode: '61',
    signUpFields: [
        {
            label: 'Please enter your username',
            key: 'username',
            placeholder: 'username',
            required: true,
            displayOrder: 1,
            type: 'string'
        },
```

7. We must change the order of the password so that it sits below the username. This tells the user that they can use their username and password to log in instead of their email:

```
    {
        label: 'Please enter a strong password',
        key: 'password',
        placeholder: '********',
        required: true,
        displayOrder: 2,
        type: 'password'
    },
    {
        label: 'Please enter your email',
        key: 'email',
        placeholder: 'abc@domain.com',
        required: true,
        displayOrder: 3,
        type: 'string'
    },
    {
        label: 'Please enter your mobile number',
        key: 'phone_number',
        placeholder: 'mobile number',
        required: false,
        displayOrder: 4,
        type: 'string'
    }
  ]
};
export default App;
```

OK; try to run the app again and call either the `yarn ios` command if you are using macOS or `yarn android` if you are not using macOS:

1. Click the **Sign Up** button on the React Native or Expo app:

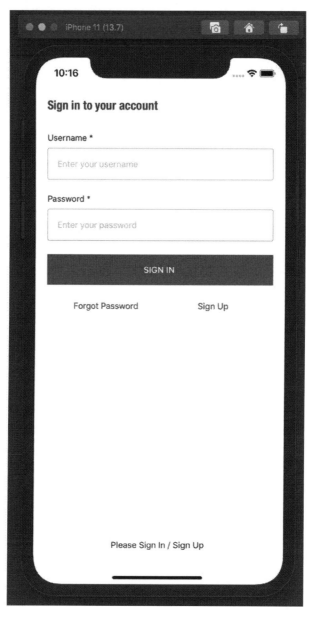

Figure 4.14 – Sign in to your account screen

2. Fill in the sign-up form with a unique username, a strong password that contains at least 8 characters, a working email address, and a mobile number, which we will set to **optional**, without the asterisk. This asterisk (*) tells the user that we have set the field to required. Press the **SIGN UP** button once you have filled in the form:

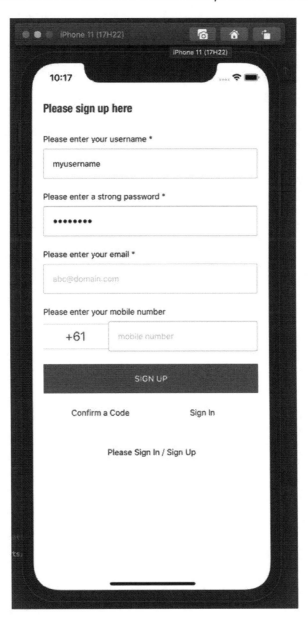

Figure 4.15 – Please sign up here screen

3. Now, wait for the confirmation code to arrive in your inbox, and then copy and paste the 6-digit code into the **Confirmation Code** field. The **Username** field should be pre-filled for you already, so press the **Confirm** button when you are ready:

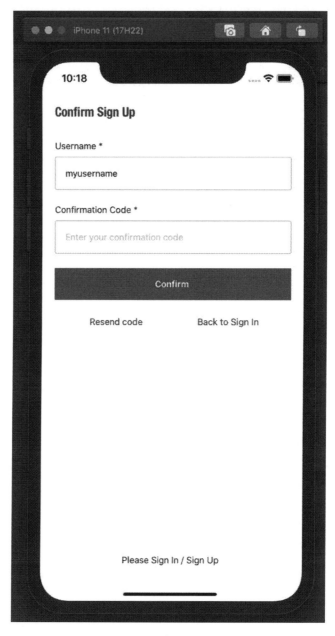

Figure 4.16 – Confirm Sign Up screen

Once you are done, the app will take you back to the sign-in screen instead of the content screen. This is because the sign-up flow is a bit different between the Amplify ReactJS library and the Amplify React Native library. In the next section, we will show you how to sign in and create the **Sign out** button for the user to sign out.

Signing in and out of the Expo and React Native apps

Now that we have created the user successfully, we can go to the AWS Cognito console to check out the user that has been created in the user pool:

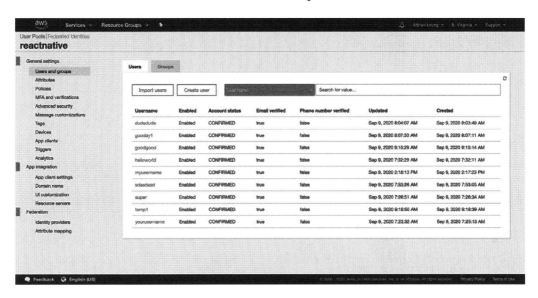

Figure 4.17 – Cognito user pool

As you can see, with just a few lines of code, we have integrated the entire authentication flow. Now, let's try to sign in with one of the users that we have created:

1. We will sign in with the last user that we have created. If you've forgotten the password, you can click on the **Forgot Password** button to retrieve it. We will show you how to do this because it is a very important self-help feature that most users will use when they forget their password. Let's press the **Forgot Password** button:

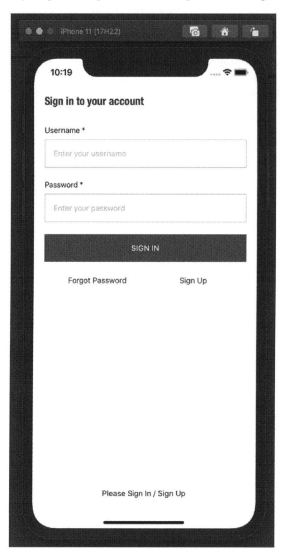

Figure 4.18 – Sign in to your account screen – pressing the Forgot Password button

2. Enter the username that you forgot the password for and then press the **SEND** button:

Figure 4.19 – Reset your password screen

3. If we enter an incorrect confirmation code, a warning message will appear, stating **Invalid verification code provided, please try again**:

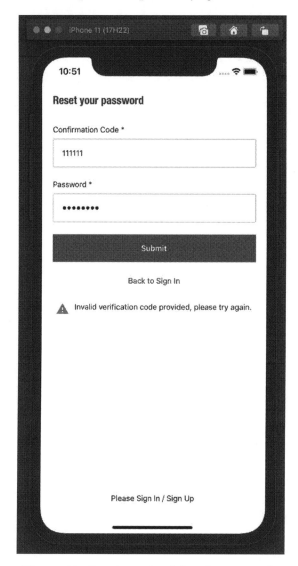

Figure 4.20 – Entering an invalid confirmation code

4. Grab the confirmation code from your email and then enter a new **password**. Press the **Submit** button when you are ready:

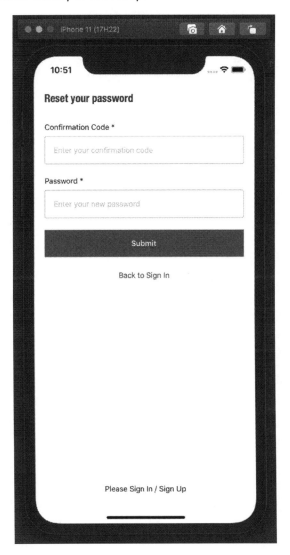

Figure 4.21 – Confirming your password

5. You will be redirected back to the sign-in screen if your **confirmation code** is correct and your **password** has been accepted. Now, enter the username and the newly created password and try to log in again:

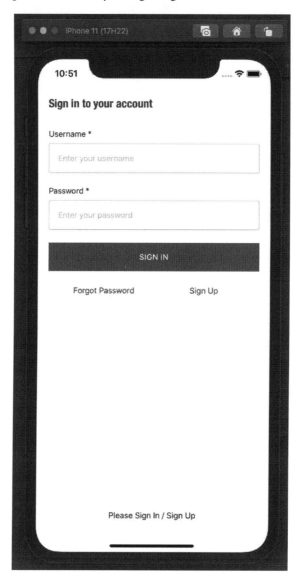

Figure 4.22 – Confirming your password

6. Once you have logged in successfully, you will see the welcome message, along with your username:

Figure 4.23 – Welcome message after logging in

7. Let's add the **Sign out** button to the code so that the user can log out. This will reset the user and their authentication state. At the same time, we can test the live update feature with Expo and React Native. Add the following code to the App.tsx file:

```
<View style={styles.container}>
    <Text>Good day, {(authState && user) ? user.
    username :
    'mate'}</Text>
    <Button title="Sign out" onPress={() => {
       Auth.signOut().then(
          () => {
             setAuthState(null);
             setUser(null);
          }
       ).catch((info: any) => console.log("Info: ",
       info));
    }} />
</View>
```

8. As soon as you save the App.tsx file, the app will be automatically reloaded. Thanks to the live update feature of React Native and Expo, you should be able to see the **Sign out** button being added to the screen, as follows:

Figure 4.24 – Sign out button

If you click on the **Sign out** button, you will be taken back to the **Sign in** screen. With that, we have implemented the entire authentication flow with just a few lines of code!

Summary

Over the course of this chapter, we have learned about how to integrate the Amplify UI with the Amplify authentication backend, which is powered by the AWS Cognito service. If you followed all three exercises for ReactJS, React Native, and Expo, you should realize that the code between the three different variations is very similar. Hopefully, you are having fun so far.

In the next chapter, we are going to look at something even more exciting, which is creating a blog post with Amplify GraphQL. We will see the magic of the GraphQL API and why it is a great way to replace the traditional RESTful API!

5
Creating a Blog Post with Amplify GraphQL

In this chapter, we will be covering a very important part of creating an **Amplify app**; that is, letting users store and query their data with GraphQL. Back in the days before the GraphQL API existed, we had the RESTful API, which did not have a common standard for how to manipulate or query data. It was all up to the backend developers, which caused more delays during development. GraphQL removed the complexity of the API schema for frontend developers.

GraphQL standardizes the API schema, thus making it easy to define as a common practice and standard. Therefore, if you or your development team adopt GraphQL as your middle tier to interact between the frontend app and the backend business layers, it can speed up the development time and remove the dependency of waiting for both sides. The Amplify CLI can help you generate the GraphQL code based on the GraphQL data model schema that you define. We will learn how to do this by covering the following topics:

- Creating a blog post with a Mutation
- Finding a blog post with a Query
- Getting real-time updates with Subscriptions

We will cover these topics for the ReactJS, Expo, and React Native projects.

Technical requirements

To complete this chapter, you must have completed the exercises found in the previous chapters. This will help understand how to create a blog post with Amplify GraphQL. Make sure that you have installed and configured the Amplify CLI as well. You can download the file from the following link: `https://github.com/PacktPublishing/Rapid-Application-Development-with-AWS-Amplify/tree/master/ch5`.

Since we will be writing GraphQL code, we will need to install the GraphQL extension with a development tool such as **Visual Studio Code** (**VSCode**). You can go to the extensions marketplace by clicking on the grid icon on the left-hand side menu. Then, search for the `graphql` extension for GraphQL syntax highlighting and validation.

Click on the **Install** button at the top. If you choose an extension with many search results, such as GraphQL, always pick the one with the most stars and downloads:

Figure 5.1 – GraphQL extension for VSCode

Once you have installed the **GraphQL** extension, you can open the `schema.graphql` file in the `amplify/backend/api/projectname` folder, which can be found in the project directory, to see that the syntax has been highlighted in different colors, as follows:

```
type Todo @model {
    id: ID!
    name: String!
    description: String
}
```

Now, we are ready to dive into the next section, which is all about creating a blog post with **Mutation**.

> **Important note**
>
> If you encounter 100% CPU usage with VSCode on macOS, which is still a known issue (`https://github.com/microsoft/vscode/issues/101555`) at the time of writing this book, you can go to the VSC website (`https://code.visualstudio.com/`), click on the down arrow drop-down button on the home page to download, and install the **Insiders Edition**.

Creating a blog post with Mutation for the ReactJS app

In this section, we will be creating a blog post with Mutation. Mutation is all about asking for specific fields in objects to create and manipulate data in GraphQL. Let's look at how to do this.

First, let's create a simple data model for a blog post. Edit the `schema.graphql` file in the `amplify/backend/api/api-name/` directory by using the following code:

```
type Post @model @key(fields: ["title"]) {
    id: ID!
    title: String!
    content: String!
}
```

The `id` parameter is a unique identifier that's assigned to each blog post to help us differentiate between them. If we put an exclamation mark (`!`) next to the type of the parameter, this means it cannot be null; that is, it cannot be empty when it is stored in the database, which is DynamoDB in our case. DynamoDB instances, tables, and connections will be generated automatically in the next step. Both the `title` and `content` parameters are necessary for the blog post, so they cannot be empty.

Once you have saved the `schema.graphql` file, please call the `amplify push` command in your Terminal to update the GraphQL API backend and generate the GraphQL code with the following settings:

```
amplify push

✔ Successfully pulled backend environment dev from the cloud.


Current Environment: dev

| Category | Resource name      | Operation | Provider plugin  |
| -------- | ------------------ | --------- | ---------------- |
| Api      | reactjsapp         | Update    | awscloudformation |
| Hosting  | amplifyhosting     | No Change | awscloudformation |
| Auth     | reactjsappxxxxxxxx | No Change | awscloudformation |

? Are you sure you want to continue? Yes
GraphQL schema compiled successfully.
Do you want to update code for your updated GraphQL API Yes
? Do you want to generate GraphQL statements (queries,
mutations and subscription) based on your schema types?
This will overwrite your current graphql queries, mutations and
subscriptions Yes
⠼ Updating resources in the cloud. This may take a few
minutes...
✔ Generated GraphQL operations successfully and saved at src/
graphql
✔ Code generated successfully and saved in file src/API.ts
✔ All resources are updated in the cloud
GraphQL endpoint: https://xxxxxxxxxxxxxxxxxxx.appsync-api.
us-east-1.amazonaws.com/graphql
GraphQL API KEY: xxx-xxxxxxxxxxxxxxxxxxxx
```

The GraphQL code has been generated by the Amplify CLI based on the model that we just created in the `src/graphql` folder:

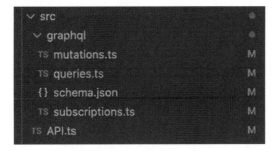

Figure 5.2 – Autogenerated GraphQL operations and API code

Let's open the `mutations.ts` file to see the code that has been generated by the Amplify CLI based on the `Post` model that we just created:

```
/* tslint:disable */
/* eslint-disable */
// this is an auto generated file. This will be overwritten

export const createPost = /* GraphQL */ `
  mutation CreatePost(
    $input: CreatePostInput!
    $condition: ModelPostConditionInput
  ) {
    createPost(input: $input, condition: $condition) {
      id
      title
      description
      _version
      _deleted
      _lastChangedAt
      createdAt
      updatedAt
      owner
    }
  }
`;
export const updatePost = /* GraphQL */ `
  mutation UpdatePost(
    $input: UpdatePostInput!
    $condition: ModelPostConditionInput
  ) {
    updatePost(input: $input, condition: $condition) {
      id
```

Figure 5.3 – Mutations

The Amplify CLI generated three methods for us: `createPost`, `updatePost`, and `deletePost`. These are the Mutation GraphQL operations for creating, updating and deleting a post on the database. All we need to do is to call the autogenerated methods to access the backend, which saves us heaps of time.

Here, we will create a web app interface as an example for the user to create a blog post. Open the `App.css` file in the project directory and perform the following steps:

1. Import the `Oswald` font from Google Fonts (`https://fonts.google.com/`) as the typography for the web app:

```css
@import url("https://fonts.googleapis.com/
css2?family=Oswald");
* {
    font-family: "Oswald", serif;
}
```

2. Set the `container` CSS class with a fixed width of `400` pixels so that it will look consistent when the user resizes the browser:

```css
.container {
    width: 400px;
    margin: 0 auto;
    display: flex;
    flex: 1;
    flex-direction: column;
    justify-content: center;
    padding-top: 20px;
}

section * {
    width: 100%;
}

.post {
    margin-bottom: 15px;
}
```

3. Set the `input` and `textarea` elements with fixed `width` and `padding` values that add up to exactly `400` pixels. This means that these elements will have the same width as the `container` class element:

```
input {
    border: none;
    background-color: #ddd;
    margin-bottom: 10px;
    font-size: 18px;
    border: none;
    padding: 10px;
    width: 380px;
}

textarea {
    border: none;
    background-color: #ddd;
    margin-bottom: 10px;
    font-size: 18px;
    height: 70px;
    border: none;
    padding: 10px;
    width: 380px;
}
```

4. Set the `font-weight` parameter of the `create-button` class to `bold` so that it is more obvious to the user:

```
.create-button {
    font-weight: bold;
    width: 100%;
    display: block;
}

.post-title {
    font-size: 20px;
    font-weight: bold;
}
```

```css
.post-content {
    margin-bottom: 0;
}
```

5. Initially, set the various parameters of the button element, such as its font size, padding, margins, and so on, with the same values to keep the buttons consistent across the app:

```css
button {
    background-color: red;
    color: white;
    outline: none;
    font-size: 18px;
    padding: 12px 0px;
    margin-top: 10px;
    margin-bottom: 50px;
    border: none;
}
```

6. Change the **Update** and **Delete** button styles so that they have a lighter background, smaller font size, and white text that appears to be less obvious to the user:

```css
.update-button,
.delete-button {
    background-color: gray;
    color: white;
    width: 100px;
    border: none;
    font-size: 12px;
}
```

7. The **Update** button will stay on the left while we use the `float` parameter to put the `delete` button on the right-hand side. This ensures that the buttons appear side by side with some space in-between them on the app:

```css
.delete-button {
    float: right;
}
```

Save the CSS file. Now, we can start editing the App.jsx file.

8. Import the `React` and `Amplify` libraries into the `App.jsx` file with the newly generated GraphQL code:

```
import React, { useEffect, useState, SetStateAction }
from "react";
import "./App.css";
import Amplify, { API, graphqlOperation } from
"aws-amplify";
import * as mutations from "./graphql/mutations";
import * as queries from "./graphql/queries";
import awsExports from "./aws-exports";
Amplify.configure(awsExports);


const App = () => {
  const defaultPostState = { id: "", title: "", content:
  "" };
```

9. Create the `postState` object, for storing the information from the input elements, and the `posts` array, for storing the blog posts that are being fetched from the database:

```
// Post
const [postState, setPostState] =
useState(defaultPostState);
const [posts, setPosts] = useState([]);
```

10. Create a `createSectionState` object to store the state of the show and hide statuses of `Create post section`. Set it to `true` so that `Create post section` will be visible by default:

```
// Create post section
const [createSectionState, setCreateSectionState] =
useState(true);
```

11. Create a `updateSectionState` object to store the state of the show and hide statuses of `Update post section`. Set it to `false` so that `Create post section` will be hidden by default:

```
// Update post section
const [updateSectionState, setUpdateSectionState] =
useState(false);
```

12. Call the `fetchPosts` method every time the page is refreshed by using the `useEffect` hook:

```
useEffect(() => {
  fetchPosts();
}, []);
```

The `fetchPosts` method will try to fetch the list of `posts` records from DynamoDB through the Amplify GraphQL API. It will set `posts` to the `posts` array if it was fetched successfully; otherwise, it will show the following error in the console:

```
const fetchPosts = async (): Promise<any> => {
  try {
    console.log("fetching posts");
    const postData: any = await API.graphql(
      graphqlOperation(queries.listPosts)
    );
    const posts: any = postData.data.listPosts.items;
    setPosts(posts);
  } catch (err) {
    console.log("error fetching posts: ", err);
  }
};

const setInput = (key: any, value: any): any => {
  setPostState({ ...postState, [key]: value });
};
```

13. Create a `refresh` method to refresh the page:

```
const refresh = () => {
  useState({});
};
```

14. The `createPost` method is used to create a new `post` record in the database based on the user inputs from the `title` input field and the `content` input field:

```
const createPost = async (): Promise<any> => {
  try {
```

```
      if (!postState.title || !postState.content) return;
      const post = { ...postState };
      console.log("creating post", post);
      const result = await API.graphql(
        graphqlOperation(mutations.createPost, {
          input: { title: post.title, content: post.
          content },
        })
      );
      setPosts([...posts, post] as
      SetStateAction<never[]>);
      setPostState(defaultPostState);
      console.log("created post", result);
    } catch (err: any) {
      console.log("error creating post:", err);
    }
  };
```

The updatePost method also updates the post that was selected by the user:

```
const updatePost = async (): Promise<any> => {
  try {
      if (!postState.title || !postState.content) return;
      const post = { ...postState };
      console.log("updating post", post);
```

15. We can provide the post id when we want to update a specific post:

```
      const result = await API.graphql(
        graphqlOperation(mutations.updatePost, {
          input: {
            id: post.id,
            title: post.title,
            content: post.content,
          },
        })
      );
```

16. Hide the **Update** section and show the **Create post** section when the update is successful:

```
        setUpdateSectionState(false);
        setCreateSectionState(true);
        console.log("updated post", result);
        setPostState(defaultPostState);
        refresh();
      } catch (err: any) {
        console.log("error updating post:", err);
      }
    };
```

17. The `deletePost` method is used to delete a specific post. To delete a specific post, we have to provide its unique `post id`:

```
    const deletePost = async (postID: string): Promise<any>
    => {
      try {
        if (!postID) return;
        console.log("deleting post", postID);
        const result = await API.graphql(
          graphqlOperation(mutations.deletePost, {
            input: {
              id: postID,
            },
          })
        );
        console.log("deleted post", result);
        refresh();
      } catch (err: any) {
        console.log("error deleting post:", err);
      }
    };

    return (
      <div>
        <div className="container">
```

18. Show the **Create post** section by default, along with the `title` input field, content text area, and the create post submit `button` element, which indicates that it is ready for users to create new posts:

```
{createSectionState === true ? (
    <section className="create-section">
        <h2>Create Post</h2>
        <input
            onChange={(event) => setInput("title",
            event.target.value)}
            value={postState.title}
            placeholder="Title"
        />
        <textarea
            onChange={(event) => setInput("content",
            event.target.value)}
            value={postState.content}
            placeholder="Content"
        />
        <button className="create-button"
          onClick={createPost}>
            Create
        </button>
    </section>
) : null}
```

19. Show the **Update post** section when the user wants to update an existing post by clicking the **Update** button of the specific post:

```
{updateSectionState === true ? (
    <section className="update-section">
        <h2>Update Post</h2>
        <input
            onChange={(event) => setInput("title",
            event.target.value)}
            value={postState.title}
            placeholder="Title"
        />
```

```
        <textarea
          onChange={ (event) => setInput ("content",
          event.target.value) }
          value={postState.content}
          placeholder="Content"
        />
        <button className="create-button"
          onClick={updatePost}>
          Update
        </button>
      </section>
    ) : null}
```

20. Now, let's display the posts that we fetched from the backend. Here, we will inject the **Update** button of each post, which will show the **Update** section so that the user can update a specific post, and the **Delete** button, which will trigger the deletePost method when it's clicked:

```
{posts.map((post: any, index: any) => (
  <div key={post.id ? post.id : index}
    className="post">
    <label className="post-title">{post.title}</
    label>
    <p className="post-content">{post.content}</
    p>
    <button
      className="update-button"
      onClick={ () => {
        setPostState(post);
        setCreateSectionState(false);
        setUpdateSectionState(true);
      }}
    >
      Update
    </button>
    <button
      className="delete-button"
```

```
            onClick={() => {
                deletePost(post.id);
            }}
        >
            Delete
        </button>
    </div>
    ))}
  </div>
 </div>
 );
};

export default App;
```

Let's run the ReactJS web app by calling the `yarn start` command in our Terminal:

1. We will see the **Create Post** screen, along with a big red **Create** button that is
    screaming *click me, click me*:

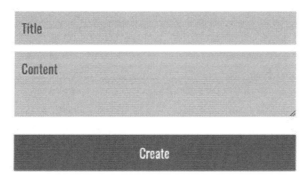

Figure 5.4 – Create Post screen

2.   Try creating a few posts to test the *Create* feature by filling the **Title** and **Content** areas and hitting the **Create** button:

Figure 5.5 – Creating a few posts

3.   If you click on the gray **Update** button under **First post content**, the *update* section will be replaced with the *create* section, where you can update the **Title** and **Content** areas and then hit the big red **Update** button:

Update Post

This is my first post~~~

Revised first post content

Update

This is my first post

First post content

Update   Delete

This is my second post

Second post content

Update   Delete

Figure 5.6 – Updating a post

You should be able to see the page being refreshed and the first post being updated, as follows:

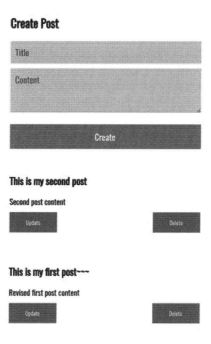

Create Post

Title

Content

Create

This is my second post

Second post content

Update   Delete

This is my first post~~~

Revised first post content

Update   Delete

Figure 5.7 – Updated posts

4. Let's click the **Delete** button under **Second post content**. You will see the page being refreshed and the second post being removed:

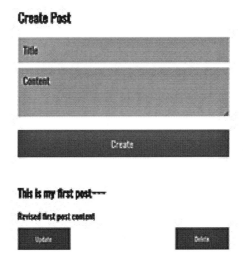

Figure 5.8 – We have deleted a post

In this section, we learned about the basic operations of mutations, which are to create, update, and delete posts. In the next section, we will understand how to use **Queries** to search for posts.

Finding a blog post with Query with ReactJS

In this section, we will be finding blog posts that the user created with Query. Query helps us look up specific records in the database with GraphQL. Let's get started:

1. Let's open the schema.graphql file again and add the following code to it. We will add the @key directive field, called title, as the primary key and index of the DynamoDB table, called Post. This means that the user can find the post that they want by using a case-sensitive keyword from the title:

```
type Post @model @key(fields: ["title"]) {
  id: ID!
  title: String!
  content: String!
}
```

Call the `amplify push` command in your Terminal to update the GraphQL backend on the cloud. Once it's updated, open the `App.jsx` file.

2. Add the following `findPosts` method below the `deletePost` method and above the `return` section of the code block. This method will list all the posts with a title that contains the keyword that was searched for:

```
const findPosts = async (title: string): Promise<any> =>
{
    try {
        console.log("finding posts:", title);
        const postData: any = await API.graphql(
            graphqlOperation(queries.listPosts, {
                filter: {
                    title: {
                        contains: title,
                    },
                },
            })
        );
        console.log("found posts:");
        const posts: any = postData.data.listPosts.items;
        setPosts(posts);
    } catch (err) {
        console.log("error finding posts ", err);
    }
};
```

3. Add the `input` tag code right below the first `container` `div` line of code in the `return` section, as follows. This will call the `findPosts` method when you are typing in the search field:

```
<div className="container">
    <input
        className="find"
        type="search"
        onChange={(event) => findPosts(event.target.
        value)}
        placeholder="Find post by title"
    />
```

4. Now, run the `yarn start` command in your Terminal again. You will see that the app has been updated with a **Find post by title** search bar, as shown in the following screenshot:

Figure 5.9 – Find post by title search bar

5. Let's create a few more posts with different titles and content, as follows:

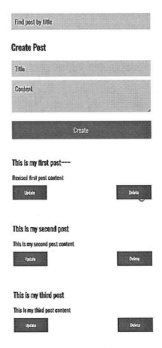

Figure 5.10 – Creating a few more posts

6.   Enter the unique post keyword in the search bar, which is `third` in our case:

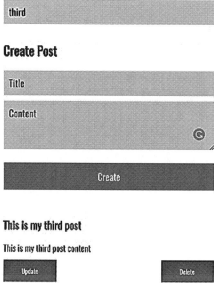

Figure 5.11 – Searching for the post with a keyword

You will see the posts appearing and disappearing while you are typing in real time. This happens because whenever a change is made in the search bar, a search is performed. If the keyword is common within a few posts, then you will see a few posts as a result.

So far, we have learned how to use Mutations to manipulate data and Queries alongside filtering to look up data. Next, we will learn how to get real-time updates about our posts whenever a change is made with Subscriptions.

Getting real-time updates with Subscriptions with ReactJS

In this section, we will show you how to use **Subscriptions** in GraphQL. Subscriptions are used to query the database and listen to changes in the data to provide instant updates when that happens. They do this by maintaining an active connection with the database. Subscriptions are useful for tasks such as producing real-time notifications when something has changed in the database.

Let's open the App.jsx file and add the following code:

1. Import the autogenerated subscriptions library at the top of the App.jsx file, as follows:

```
import React, { useEffect, useState, SetStateAction }
from "react";
import "./App.css";
import Amplify, { API, graphqlOperation } from
"aws-amplify";
import * as mutations from "./graphql/mutations";
import * as queries from "./graphql/queries";
import * as subscriptions from "./graphql/subscriptions";
import awsExports from "./aws-exports";
```

2. Add the following code block within the useEffect hook. This will subscribe to actions such as creating a new post, updating an existing post, and deleting an existing post. If there's a change in the createSubscription method, it will trigger the fetchPosts method. All the subscriptions will be unsubscribed from during the unmount event of the page:

```
useEffect(() => {
    const fetchPosts = async (): Promise<any> => {
        try {
            console.log("fetching posts");
            const postData: any = await API.graphql(
                graphqlOperation(queries.listPosts)
            );
            const posts: any = postData.data.listPosts.items;
            setPosts(posts);
        } catch (err) {
            console.log("error fetching posts: ", err);
        }
    };

    const createSubscription: any = API.graphql(
        graphqlOperation(subscriptions.onCreatePost)
    );
```

```
createSubscription.subscribe({
  next: (postData: any) => {
    console.log("onCreatePost", postData);
    fetchPosts();
  },
});

const updateSubscription: any = API.graphql(
  graphqlOperation(subscriptions.onUpdatePost)
);
updateSubscription.subscribe({
  next: (postData: any) => {
    console.log("onUpdatePost", postData);
    fetchPosts();
  },
});

const deleteSubscription: any = API.graphql(
  graphqlOperation(subscriptions.onDeletePost)
);
deleteSubscription.subscribe({
  next: (postData: any) => {
    console.log("onDeletePost", postData);
    fetchPosts();
  },
});

return () => {
  createSubscription.unsubscribe();
  updateSubscription.unsubscribe();
  deleteSubscription.unsubscribe();
};
}, []);
```

3. Run the `yarn start` command in your Terminal to test the app again. This time, open two browsers and input the same testing URL, `http://localhost:3000`, as follows:

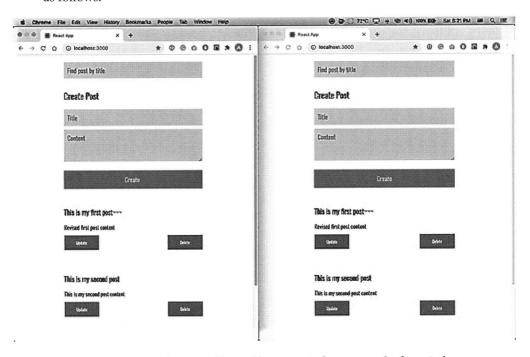

Figure 5.12 – Launching an additional browser window next to the first window

4. Let's update the first post that we created by clicking the **Update** button of the first post. Make some changes in the **Update post** section and then hit the big red **Update** button to see the real-time changes in both browser windows, as follows:

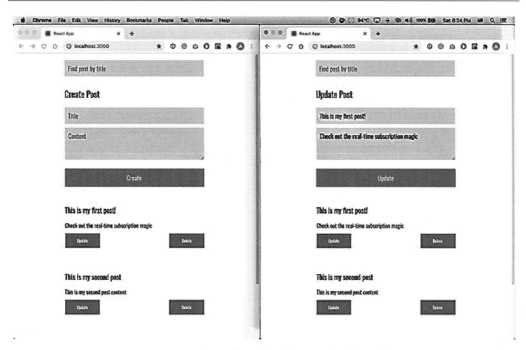

Figure 5.13 – Both windows have been updated in real time

Now, you can try to create a new post or delete an existing post to see the subscription in action.

So far, we've learned about the power of GraphQL in terms of Mutations, Queries, and Subscriptions, all of which can be applied easily in many situations. Many apps require us to basic operations surrounding data manipulation, including querying and subscribing to changes that have been made to database records; GraphQL covers all these bases.

In the next three sections, we will do the same thing for the Expo and React Native apps.

Creating a blog post with Mutations for Expo and React Native

In this section, we will show you how to use Mutations to create a blog post with Expo and React Native, as we did with the ReactJS version previously. Mutations ask for specific fields in objects to create and manipulate data in GraphQL. Let's get started:

1. Open the `AppStyles.ts` file and enter the following styling code for the Native components:

```
import { StyleSheet } from "react-native";
export default StyleSheet.create({
  safeArea: { flex: 1, marginHorizontal: 16 },
  container: { flex: 1, justifyContent: "flex-start",
  padding:
  20 },
  title: { fontSize: 22, fontWeight: "bold",
  marginBottom: 10
  },
  input: { height: 50, backgroundColor: "#ddd",
  marginBottom:
  10, padding: 10 },
  textArea: {
    backgroundColor: "#ddd",
    padding: 10,
    height: 70,
    marginBottom: 10,
  },
  button: {
    backgroundColor: "red",
    color: "white",
    fontWeight: "bold",
    padding: 10,
    textAlign: "center",
    fontSize: 15,
  },
  scrollView: {
```

```
        marginTop: 20,
    },
    post: { marginBottom: 15 },
    postTitle: { fontSize: 18, fontWeight: "bold" },
    postContent: { fontSize: 16, marginBottom: 10 },
    postUpdate: { fontSize: 12, width: "50%", textAlign:
"center" },
    postDelete: { fontSize: 12, width: "50%", textAlign:
"center" },
});
```

Now that we've updated the theme of the app, we will add some code to the App.
tsx file to create the actual app.

2. Import the React libraries and React Native components:

```
import React, { useEffect, useState, SetStateAction }
from "react";
import {
    View,
    Text,
    SafeAreaView,
    ScrollView,
    TextInput,
    Button,
} from "react-native";
import styles from "./AppStyles";
import Amplify, { API, graphqlOperation } from
"aws-amplify";
import * as mutations from "./src/graphql/mutations";
import * as queries from "./src/graphql/queries";
import * as subscriptions from "./src/graphql/
subscriptions";
import awsExports from "./aws-exports";
Amplify.configure(awsExports);
```

```
const App = () => {
   const defaultPostState = { id: "", title: "", content:
"" };
   // Post
   const [postState, setPostState] =
   useState(defaultPostState);
   const [posts, setPosts] = useState([]);
   // Create post section
   const [createSectionState, setCreateSectionState] =
   useState(true);
   // Update post section
   const [updateSectionState, setUpdateSectionState] =
   useState(false);

   useEffect(() => {
     fetchPosts();
   }, []);
```

3. The `fetchPosts` method is used to fetch the posts on the screen at any time:

```
   const fetchPosts = async (): Promise<any> => {
     try {
       console.log("fetching posts");
       const postData: any = await API.graphql(
         graphqlOperation(queries.listPosts)
       );
       const posts: any = postData.data.listPosts.items;
       setPosts(posts);
     } catch (err) {
       console.log("error fetching posts: ", err);
     }
   };

   const setInput = (key: any, value: any): any => {
     setPostState({ ...postState, [key]: value });
   };
```

4. The `createPost` method is used to create the post with the `title` and the `content` parameters of the `postState` object:

```
const createPost = async (): Promise<any> => {
  try {
    if (!postState.title || !postState.content) return;
    const post = { ...postState };
    console.log("creating post", post);
    const result = await API.graphql(
      graphqlOperation(mutations.createPost, {
        input: { title: post.title, content: post.
        content },
      })
    );
    setPosts([...posts, post] as
    SetStateAction<never[]>);
    setPostState(defaultPostState);
    console.log("created post", result);
  } catch (err: any) {
    console.log("error creating post:", err);
  }
};
```

5. The `updatedPost` method is used to update the post with an additional ID as an identifier:

```
const updatePost = async (): Promise<any> => {
  try {
    if (!postState.title || !postState.content) return;
    const post = { ...postState };
    console.log("updating post", post);
    const result = await API.graphql(
      graphqlOperation(mutations.updatePost, {
        input: {
          id: post.id,
          title: post.title,
          content: post.content,
        },
```

```
            })
          );
          setUpdateSectionState(false);
          setCreateSectionState(true);
          console.log("updated post", result);
          setPostState(defaultPostState);
      } catch (err: any) {
          console.log("error updating post:", err);
      }
  };
```

6. The `deletePost` method is used to delete the post with a unique ID:

```
    const deletePost = async (postID: string): Promise<any>
=> {
      try {
          if (!postID) return;
          console.log("deleting post", postID);
          const result = await API.graphql(
            graphqlOperation(mutations.deletePost, {
              input: {
                id: postID,
              },
            })
          );
          console.log("deleted post", result);
      } catch (err: any) {
          console.log("error deleting post:", err);
      }
  };
```

7. The `SafeAreaView` element is a safe area for displaying content on various devices. If you have a smartphone with a notch because of the iPhone X's design trend, you don't want the content of the app being blocked by the notch. So, by creating the app inside this safe area, we can ensure that nothing will go under the notch, if there is one:

```
    return (
        <SafeAreaView style={styles.safeArea}>
```

```
<View style={styles.container}>
  {createSectionState ? (
    <View>
      <Text style={styles.title}>Create Post</Text>
      <TextInput
        onChangeText={(val) => setInput("title",
        val)}
        style={styles.input}
        value={postState.title}
        placeholder="Title"
      />
      <TextInput
        onChangeText={(val) => setInput("content",
        val)}
        style={styles.textArea}
        value={postState.content}
        placeholder="Content"
      />
      <Text style={styles.button}
      onPress={createPost}>
        Create Post
      </Text>
    </View>
  ) : null}
```

8. The **Update** section is hidden by default; it will only appear when the user clicks the **Update** button of a specific post:

```
{updateSectionState ? (
  <View>
    <Text style={styles.title}>Update Post</Text>
    <TextInput
      onChangeText={(val) => setInput("title",
      val)}
      style={styles.input}
      value={postState.title}
      placeholder="Title"
    />
```

```
            <TextInput
                onChangeText={(val) => setInput("content",
                val)}
                style={styles.textArea}
                value={postState.content}
                placeholder="Content"
            />
            <Text style={styles.button}
            onPress={updatePost}>
                Update Post
            </Text>
        </View>
    ) : null}
```

9. We added a `ScrollView` element for the posts because if you have a lot of posts on the screen, you want the posts to be scrollable so that you can go through them all one by one by swiping the screen:

```
    <ScrollView style={styles.scrollView}>
        {posts.map((post: any, index: any) => (
            <View key={post.id ? post.id : index}
            style={styles.post}>
                <Text style={styles.postTitle}>
                {post.title}</Text>
                <Text style={styles.postContent}>
                {post.content}</Text>
```

10. In terms of styling the React Native and Expo apps, if you want two buttons sitting side by side, you need to create a `View` element as a `container` to wrap two buttons and set its `flexDirection` parameter to `row`:

```
            <View style={{ flexDirection: "row" }}>
                <Text
                    style={styles.postUpdate}
                    onPress={() => {
```

```
                setPostState(post);
                setUpdateSectionState(true);
                setCreateSectionState(false);
              }}
            >
              Update
            </Text>
            <Text
              style={styles.postDelete}
              onPress={() => {
                deletePost(post.id);
              }}
            >
              Delete
            </Text>
          </View>
        </View>
      ))}
      </ScrollView>
    </View>
  </SafeAreaView>
  );
};

export default App;
```

Run the `yarn ios` or `yarn android` command in your Terminal, depending on which OS you are using, to test the app. Try to create a few posts and edit them, as follows:

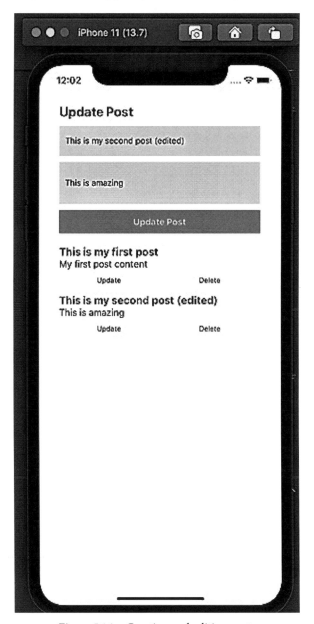

Figure 5.14 – Creating and editing posts

With that, we have the Expo and React Native apps working with the **Create** and **Update** posts features. In the next section, we will learn how to use Query to search for posts.

Finding a blog post with Query for Expo and React Native

In this section, we will learn how to search for posts with a search bar and a simple GraphQL Query. Query looks for specific records in the database with GraphQL. Let's get started:

1. Open the `App.tsx` file and add the following `findPosts` code anywhere above the `return` code block:

```
const findPosts = async (title: string): Promise<any> =>
{
    try {
        console.log("finding posts:", title);
        const postData: any = await API.graphql(
            graphqlOperation(queries.listPosts, {
                filter: {
                    title: {
                        contains: title,
                    },
                },
            })
        );
        console.log("found posts:");
        const posts: any = postData.data.listPosts.items;
        setPosts(posts);
    } catch (err) {
        console.log("error finding posts ", err);
    }
};
```

2. We will add the search bar with the `TextInput` element code right below `SafeAreaView` and the first `View`, as shown in the following code:

```
<SafeAreaView style={styles.safeArea}>
    <View style={styles.container}>
        <TextInput
            onChangeText={(val) => findPosts(val)}
```

```
                    style={styles.input}
                    placeholder="Search"
        />
```

Now, run the `yarn ios` or `yarn android` command, depending on which OS you are using, to test the search feature. Do this by entering the **second** keyword in the search field. This will show you the post that has **second** as a keyword in the search results:

Figure 5.15 – Searching for a post by title

With that, we have got the search feature working with the autogenerated GraphQL Query code. In the next section, we will learn how to use GraphQL Subscriptions to monitor changes in the data.

Getting real-time updates with Subscriptions for Expo and React Native

In this section, we will learn how to use GraphQL Subscriptions to monitor for changes. Subscriptions help us query the database and listen to changes in the data. This helps us provide instant updates as we can maintain an active connection with the database. Subscriptions are useful for tasks such as creating real-time notifications when something has changed in the database. Open the `App.tsx` file and enter the following code anywhere within the `useEffect` hook:

1. The `createSubscription` method will listen to the *create action on the database* with the autogenerated code called `onCreatePost` of the `subscriptions` object. It will do this to fetch posts when new ones are posted:

```
useEffect(() => {
    const fetchPosts = async (): Promise<any> => {
      try {
        console.log("fetching posts");
        const postData: any = await API.graphql(
          graphqlOperation(queries.listPosts)
        );
        const posts: any = postData.data.listPosts.items;
        setPosts(posts);
      } catch (err) {
        console.log("error fetching posts: ", err);
      }
    };
    fetchPosts();
    const createSubscription: any = API.graphql(
      graphqlOperation(subscriptions.onCreatePost)
    );
    createSubscription.subscribe({
      next: (postData: any) => {
        console.log("onCreatePost", postData);
```

```
        fetchPosts();
      },
    });
```

2. The updateSubscription method will listen to the *update action on the database* with the autogenerated code called onUpdatePost of the subscriptions object, in order to perform an action which is fetching posts, when there is a new post. The same thing happens with the deleteSubscription method:

```
    const updateSubscription: any = API.graphql(
      graphqlOperation(subscriptions.onUpdatePost)
    );
    updateSubscription.subscribe({
      next: (postData: any) => {
        console.log("onUpdatePost", postData);
        fetchPosts();
      },
    });


    const deleteSubscription: any = API.graphql(
      graphqlOperation(subscriptions.onDeletePost)
    );
    deleteSubscription.subscribe({
      next: (postData: any) => {
        console.log("onDeletePost", postData);
        fetchPosts();
      },
    });


    return () => {
      createSubscription.unsubscribe();
      updateSubscription.unsubscribe();
      deleteSubscription.unsubscribe();
    };
  }, []);
```

Once we've saved the file, we must run the `yarn ios` or `yarn android` command to test the `subscription` feature. If you are using a Mac, you can open the app in both iOS and Android simulators to test the `subscription` feature, as follows:

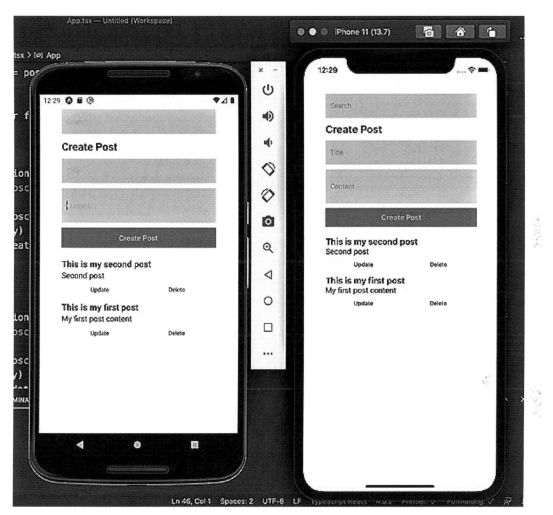

Figure 5.16 – Subscription feature on iOS and Android

In this section, we learned how to use GraphQL Subscriptions for Expo and React Native to monitor database updates – even those between iOS and Android.

Summary

In this chapter, we learned how to create a GraphQL data model, generate GraphQL API code, and how to use the Mutations, Queries, and Subscriptions features of GraphQL. Most modern websites and mobile apps could benefit from such a unified way of manipulating and querying data.

In the next chapter, we will add the Amplify Photo Picker UI as an extension to this app so that you can create a blog post with images.

6
Uploading and Sharing Photos with Amplify Storage

In this chapter, we will continue with what we built in *Chapter 5, Creating a Blog Post with Amplify GraphQL*, by adding the ability for users to upload and share photos to their blog. AWS Amplify comes with quite a few pre-built UI components that are ready to use. In this chapter, we will learn how to utilize the Photo Picker and Image components for our tutorial. Photo sharing is very common on the internet these days – it's a way to show people what you care about, not only with text but images, which gives people an idea of your life. The entire image upload and display mechanism can be quite complex for many, especially for those who are not familiar with backend technologies. AWS Amplify handles this for you behind the scenes – all you need to do is plug and play with several Amplify UI components.

In this chapter, we will cover the following topics:

- Adding the React Photo Picker UI component and Amplify Storage with ReactJS
- Sharing an image with text as a blog post with ReactJS
- Listing all the blog posts with real-time updates with ReactJS
- Adding the Photo Picker component with Amplify Storage with Expo and React Native
- Sharing an image with text as a blog post with React Native and Expo
- Listing all the blog posts with real-time updates with React Native and Expo

We will cover these points for the ReactJS, Expo, and React Native projects.

Technical requirements

To follow along with this chapter, you will need to have completed the exercises in all the previous chapters so that you can start adding photos to blog posts. You can download the file for this chapter from the following link: `https://github.com/PacktPublishing/Rapid-Application-Development-with-AWS-Amplify/tree/master/ch6`.

We will need to change the data model to the following to accommodate the user uploading image alongside the actual blog post. Once we've done this, we'll need to call the `amplify push` command to push the new changes to the cloud:

```
type Post @model @key(fields: ["title"]) {
    id: ID!
    title: String!
    content: String!
    image: String
}
```

To upload photos to the Amplify Storage backend, we will need to call the `amplify add storage` command in a Terminal. This will add Amplify Storage to the cloud's backend:

```
amplify add storage
? Please select from one of the below mentioned services:
Content (Images, audio, video, etc.)
? Please provide a friendly name for your resource that will be
used to label this category in the project: s3xxxxxxxxx
```

```
? Please provide bucket name: reactjsxxxxxxxxxxxxxxxxxxxxxxxxxxxxx
? Who should have access: Auth and guest users
? What kind of access do you want for Authenticated users?
create/update, read, delete
? What kind of access do you want for Guest users? create/
update, read, delete
? Do you want to add a Lambda Trigger for your S3 Bucket? No
Successfully updated auth resource locally.
Successfully added resource s3xxxxxxxxxx locally
If a user is part of a user pool group, run "amplify update
storage" to enable IAM group policies for CRUD operations
Some next steps:
"amplify push" builds all of your local backend resources and
provisions them in the cloud
"amplify publish" builds all of your local backend and front-
end resources (if you added hosting category) and provisions
them in the cloud
```

Call the `amplify push` command in a terminal to push the changes to the cloud's backend:

```
amplify push
✔ Successfully pulled backend environment dev from the cloud.
Current Environment: dev

| Category | Resource name   | Operation | Provider plugin   |
| -------- | --------------- | --------- | ----------------- |
| Auth     | reactjsxxxxxxx  | No Change | awscloudformation |
| Storage  | s3a1234567      | Create    | awscloudformation |
| Api      | reactjs         | No Change | awscloudformation |
? Are you sure you want to continue? Yes
⠏ Updating resources in the cloud. This may take a few
minutes...
✔ All resources are updated in the cloud
```

Now, we are ready to add the photo upload capability to our apps.

Adding the React Photo Picker UI component and Amplify Storage with ReactJS

In this section, we will learn how to add the Photo Picker UI component to the app, as well as the code that lets the user add a photo to the app through Amplify Storage. This will allow other users to see the photo through the app. Normally, we would need to write a lot of frontend and backend code to achieve this, but in this section, I will show you how to code in a minimal way. Let's get started:

1. Let's open the App.css file and add the following CSS code so that we can style the Amplify S3 Image UI component at the bottom of the CSS file:

```
amplify-s3-image {
    --width: 400px;
}
```

2. Open the App.tsx file and add the following code to it:

```
import React, { useEffect, useState, SetStateAction } from "react";
import "./App.css";
import Amplify, { API, graphqlOperation, Storage } from "aws-amplify";
import * as mutations from "./graphql/mutations";
import * as queries from "./graphql/queries";
import * as subscriptions from "./graphql/subscriptions";
import { AmplifyS3Image } from "@aws-amplify/ui-react";
import awsExports from "./aws-exports";


Amplify.configure(awsExports);


const App = () => {
    const defaultPostState = { id: "", title: "", content:
    "",
    image: "" };
    // Post
    const [postState, setPostState] =
    useState(defaultPostState);
    const [posts, setPosts] = useState([]);
```

```
// Create post section
const [createSectionState, setCreateSectionState] =
useState(true);
// Update post section
const [updateSectionState, setUpdateSectionState] =
useState(false);
```

3. Create the `img` object for storing the upload image information and the `onImageUploadChange` method for uploading the image to `Amplify Storage` directly:

```
//image upload
const [img, setImg] = useState("");
const onImageUploadChange = (event: any) => {
  const file = event.target.files[0];
  const fileName = file.name;
  const contentType =
  fileName.split(".").pop().toLowerCase();
  console.log("fileName", fileName);
  setInput("image", fileName as string);
  Storage.put(fileName, file, {
    contentType: "image/" + contentType,
  })
    .then(async (result: any) => {
```

4. Set the image with the `key` property that was stored in Amplify Storage:

```
      console.log("result.key", result.key);
      setImg((await Storage.get(result.key)) as
      string);
    })
    .catch((err) => console.error(err));
};

useEffect(() => {
  fetchPosts();
}, []);

const fetchPosts = async (): Promise<any> => {
```

```
    try {
        console.log("fetching posts");
        const postData: any = await API.graphql(
            graphqlOperation(queries.listPosts)
        );
        const posts: any = postData.data.listPosts.items;
        setPosts(posts);
    } catch (err) {
        console.log("error fetching posts: ", err);
    }
};
```

5. The `setInput` method is being used for the post object, including its ID, title, content, and the new image field:

```
const setInput = (key: any, value: any): any => {
    setPostState({ ...postState, [key]: value });
};
```

6. Add the `image` attribute as an input parameter and `post.image` as the value of the `createPost` method. This must be done as part of the `createPost` GraphQL mutation operation:

```
const createPost = async (): Promise<any> => {
    try {
        if (!postState.title || !postState.content) return;
        const post = { ...postState };
        console.log("creating post", post);
        const result = await API.graphql(
            graphqlOperation(mutations.createPost, {
                input: {
                    title: post.title,
                    content: post.content,
                    image: post.image,
                },
            })
        );
        setPosts([...posts, post] as
```

```
SetStateAction<never[]>);
        setPostState(defaultPostState);
        console.log("created post", result);
    } catch (err: any) {
        console.log("error creating post:", err);
    }
};
```

7. Add the `image` attribute as an input parameter and `post.image` as the value of the `updatePost` method. This must be done as part of the `updatePost` GraphQL mutation operation:

```
const updatePost = async (): Promise<any> => {
  try {
      if (!postState.title || !postState.content) return;
      const post = { ...postState };
      console.log("updating post", post);
      const result = await API.graphql(
        graphqlOperation(mutations.updatePost, {
          input: {
            id: post.id,
            title: post.title,
            content: post.content,
            image: post.image,
          },
        })
      );
      setUpdateSectionState(false);
      setCreateSectionState(true);
      console.log("updated post", result);
      setPostState(defaultPostState);
    } catch (err: any) {
      console.log("error updating post:", err);
    }
};
```

The `deletePost` method remains unchanged because all you need is the `id` property of the post for the GraphQL delete operation:

```
const deletePost = async (postID: string): Promise<any>
=> {
  try {
    if (!postID) return;
    console.log("deleting post", postID);
    const result = await API.graphql(
      graphqlOperation(mutations.deletePost, {
        input: {
          id: postID,
        },
      })
    );
    console.log("deleted post", result);
  } catch (err: any) {
    console.log("error deleting post:", err);
  }
};
```

`findPosts` also remains unchanged, and it will be called when we are typing into the **Find post by title** field:

```
const findPosts = async (title: string): Promise<any>
=> {
  try {
    console.log("finding posts:", title);
    const postData: any = await API.graphql(
      graphqlOperation(queries.listPosts, {
        filter: {
          title: {
            contains: title,
          },
        },
      })
    );
    console.log("found posts:");
    const posts: any = postData.data.listPosts.items;
```

```
      setPosts(posts);
    } catch (err) {
      console.log("error finding posts ", err);
    }
  };
```

The `return` section is for rendering the UI elements that the user can see:

```
    return (
      <div>
        <div className="container">
          <input
            className="find"
            type="search"
            onChange={(event) => findPosts(event.target.
            value)}
            placeholder="Find post by title"
          />
          {createSectionState === true ? (
            <section className="create-section">
              <h2>Create Post</h2>
```

8. Add the `img` tag to show the image that has been selected by the user:

```
              {img && <img src={img} alt={img}></img>}
              <input
                type="file"
                accept="image/*"
                onChange={(event) =>
                onImageUploadChange(event)}
              />
              <input
                onChange={(event) => setInput("title",
                event.target.value)}
                value={postState.title}
                placeholder="Title"
              />
              <textarea
                onChange={(event) => setInput("content",
```

```
              event.target.value)}
          value={postState.content}
          placeholder="Content"
      />
      <button className="create-button"
      onClick={createPost}>
          Create
      </button>
  </section>
) : null}
```

9. Do the same thing with the update section too; add the img tag to show the image
   that has been selected by the user:

```
{updateSectionState === true ? (
    {img && <img src={img} alt={img}></img>}
    <input
      type="file"
      accept="image/*"
      onChange={(event) =>
      onImageUploadChange(event)}
    />
    <section className="update-section">
      <h2>Update Post</h2>
      <input
        onChange={(event) => setInput("title",
        event.target.value)}
        value={postState.title}
        placeholder="Title"
      />
      <textarea
        onChange={(event) => setInput("content",
        event.target.value)}
        value={postState.content}
        placeholder="Content"
      />
      <button className="create-button"
      onClick={updatePost}>
```

```
              Update
           </button>
        </section>
     ) : null}
```

10. Add the `AmplifyS3Image` component to show the image that has been uploaded alongside `post`:

```
{posts.map((post: any, index: any) => (
   <div key={post.id ? post.id : index}
   className="post">
      <AmplifyS3Image imgKey={post.image} />
      <label className="post-title">{post.title}</
      label>
      <p className="post-content">{post.content}</
      p>
      <button
        className="update-button"
        onClick={() => {
           setPostState(post);
           setCreateSectionState(false);
           setUpdateSectionState(true);
        }}
      >
         Update
      </button>
      <button
        className="delete-button"
        onClick={() => {
           deletePost(post.id);
        }}
      >
         Delete
      </button>
   </div>
   ))}
</div>
</div>
```

```
  );
};
export default App;
```

With that, we have added the photo upload mechanism, as well as the post creation and post update features, so that your users can create a post that contains photos. This feature allows you to create typical modern websites and mobile apps, such as popular blog websites and social media apps. More importantly, you have the frontend and backend all wired up behind the scenes through Amplify. In the next section, we will learn how to create a blog post with an image by using the code that we just added to the app.

Sharing an image with text as a blog post with ReactJS

In this section, we will create a blog post with the code that we created in the previous section. Imagine that someone who has visited your website has signed up and logged in as a user and then thinks of something worth sharing. To do this, they must create a blog post. In this section, we will show you how the user will pick an image and then add a title and content, as well as click the **Create** button to ensure the functionalities are working perfectly. Let's get started:

1. First, let's call the `yarn start` command in a Terminal to run the app. Try to create a new post by uploading a photo, fill in the title and content fields, and then click the **Create** button:

Find post by title

Create Post

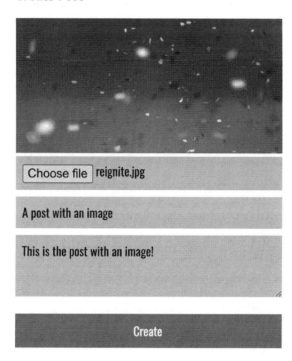

Choose file | reignite.jpg

A post with an image

This is the post with an image!

Create

This is my first post!

Check out the real-time subscription magic

Figure 6.1 – Uploading a photo during post creation

2.   You should be able to scroll down to the bottom of the page to check out the newly
created post, as shown here:

Figure 6.2 – Newly created post with an image

It is just that easy! With that, we the photo upload feature is now working. In the next
section, we will show you how to list the blog posts that we created with real-time updates
through subscriptions.

Listing all the blog posts with real-time updates with ReactJS

In this section, we will learn how to use subscriptions in our app to listen to certain events such as post creation, post update, and post delete. As soon as we call the backend through the GraphQL API to perform a task, such as creating a post, the subscribers of the `onCreatePost` event will get notified. The same will happen for post update and deletion. Let's get started:

1. Add the following code anywhere before the return section of the App.tsx file:

```
const createSubscription: any = API.graphql(
  graphqlOperation(subscriptions.onCreatePost)
);
createSubscription.subscribe({
  next: (postData: any) => {
    console.log("onCreatePost", postData);
    fetchPosts();
  },
});

const updateSubscription: any = API.graphql(
  graphqlOperation(subscriptions.onUpdatePost)
);
updateSubscription.subscribe({
  next: (postData: any) => {
    console.log("onUpdatePost", postData);
    fetchPosts();
  },
});

const deleteSubscription: any = API.graphql(
  graphqlOperation(subscriptions.onDeletePost)
);
deleteSubscription.subscribe({
  next: (postData: any) => {
    console.log("onDeletePost", postData);
    fetchPosts();
```

```
        },
    });
```

2. Let's run the `yarn start` command in a Terminal and open one more browser window, this time with the same `http://localhost:3000` URL and create a new post in it.

    You should be able to see the new post that has been created at the bottom of both browser windows, as follows:

Figure 6.3 – Newly created post with an image

As you can see, it is very simple to use the Amplify Storage and Amplify Image components to upload images and display them from the cloud. All this happens in real time. In the next section, we will do thing same thing with React Native and Expo so that you can create a mobile app with the exact same features that your website provides.

Adding the Photo Picker component with Amplify Storage with Expo and React Native

In this section, we will add the Photo Picker component to our Expo and React Native apps to let the user upload photos to Amplify Storage (an S3 Bucket). The steps will be similar between Expo and React Native, but the component will be slightly different.

To let the user upload their image to Amplify Storage, we need to add the image picker library to the project:

1. For the Expo app, install the specific image picker library that is developed by Expo called `expo-image-picker` by running the following command:

    ```
    expo install expo-image-picker
    ```

2. For the React Native app, install the community-made image called `react-native-image-picker` by running the following two commands:

    ```
    yarn add react-native-image-picker
    npx pod-install
    ```

3. Once you have installed the image picker for your React Native project, recompile the project with the `yarn ios` and `yarn android` commands to see if it works.

4. If you try to run the `yarn android` command to recompile the Android version of the React Native app, you may run into the following error. This is because the latest version of the React Native image picker library requires a minimum SDK version of 21 instead of 16:

    ```
    FAILURE: Build failed with an exception.


    * What went wrong:
    Execution failed for task ':app:processDebugManifest'.
    > Manifest merger failed : uses-sdk:minSdkVersion 16
    cannot be smaller than version 21 declared in library
    [:react-native-image-picker]
    ```

5. So, let's go to the Android folder to edit the `build.gradle` file and change the `minSdkVersion` value from `16` to `21`, as follows:

```
buildscript {
    ext {
        buildToolsVersion = "29.0.2"
        minSdkVersion = 21
        compileSdkVersion = 29
        targetSdkVersion = 29
    }
```

6. Let's try to rerun the yarn `android` command for the React Native Android project. This time, we should be able to see the app running successfully on the Android emulator.

With that, you have learned how to easily add the Photo Picker component to your React Native and Expo projects. In the next section, we will show you how to share an image with text for React Native and Expo with a step-by-step guide, just like you would normally do on social media.

Sharing an image with text as a blog post with React Native and Expo

In this section, we will learn how to let users upload images as part of a blog post to an S3 Bucket via the built-in Amplify Storage service. We will look at both the Expo and React Native projects, and point out the differences between the two. Open the `App.tsx` file in your Expo or React Native project and follow these steps:

1. First, we must import the required libraries; that is, the React and React Native UI components:

```
import React, { useEffect, useState, SetStateAction }
from "react";
import {
  View,
  Text,
  SafeAreaView,
  ScrollView,
```

```
  Image,
  TextInput
} from "react-native";
import { StatusBar } from 'expo-status-bar';
import styles from "./AppStyles";
import Amplify, { Auth, API, graphqlOperation, Storage }
from "aws-amplify";
import * as mutations from "./src/graphql/mutations";
import * as queries from "./src/graphql/queries";
import * as subscriptions from "./src/graphql/
subscriptions";
```

2. Next, we must import our image picker. This will depend on our project.

    For the React Expo project, we must import the `expo-image-picker` library:

```
Import * as ImagePicker from "expo-image-picker";
```

    For React Native, we must import the `react-native-image-picker` library:

```
import { launchImageLibrary, ImageLibraryOptions } from
'react-native-image-picker';
```

3. At this point, we must import the `S3Image` library, which is the AWS Amplify pre-built UI component for React Native. It will display the image from the S3 Bucket and reuse the code from *Chapter 5, Creating a Blog Post with Amplify GraphQL*:

```
import {S3Image} from 'aws-amplify-react-native';
import awsExports from './aws-exports';
Amplify.configure(awsExports);

const App = () => {
  const defaultPostState = { id: "", title: "", content:
"", image: "" };
  // Post
  const [postState, setPostState] =
  useState(defaultPostState);
  const [posts, setPosts] = useState([]);
```

```
    // Create post section
    const [createSectionState, setCreateSectionState] =
    useState(true);
    // Update post section
    const [updateSectionState, setUpdateSectionState] =
    useState(false);
    //image upload
    const [img, setImg] = useState("");
    useEffect(() => {
      fetchPosts();
    }, []);
```

For the *React Native Android app only*, you might want to import the `LogBox` library and call the `ignoreAllLogs` function in the app block to get rid of the error logs. It is unrelated to your app, but it's a known issue (`https://stackoverflow.com/questions/46513408/react-native-warning-setting-a-timer-for-a-long-period-of-time-how-to-loc#46513980`) with React Native:

```
import { LogBox } from 'react-native';

import awsExports from './aws-exports';
Amplify.configure(awsExports);

const App = () => {
   LogBox.ignoreAllLogs();
```

If you don't add the preceding code, you will see an error stating **Setting a timer for a long period of time** on the screen, as follows:

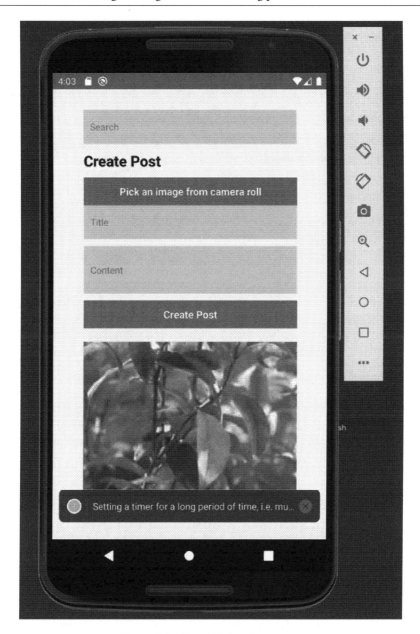

Figure 6.4 – React Native timer error

4. We will create a method here called `urlToBlob` because the upload image feature will only upload the blob to the S3 Bucket. If we don't convert the image path that is returned by the image picker from a URL into a blob, the *Amplify Storage library will upload an empty image to S3 instead*:

```
const urlToBlob = async (url:string) => {
  return new Promise((resolve, reject) => {
    var xhr = new XMLHttpRequest();
    xhr.onerror = reject;
    xhr.onreadystatechange = () => {
      if (xhr.readyState === 4) {
        resolve(xhr.response);
      }
    };
    xhr.open('GET', url);
    xhr.responseType = 'blob';
    xhr.send();
  })
}
```

5. Let's create the image upload function for both the Expo and React Native apps. You will see that the differences are minimal. I really wish that they shared the exact same library so that the Expo SDK and backend can take care of the differences. We will keep the image cropped with an aspect ratio of 4:3 and set the image quality to 0.1, which is the maximum compression we can use, to increase the image's upload speed and minimize the storage cost on S3.

    For React Expo, use the following code:

```
const onImageUploadChange = async () => {
  try {
    let imageFile = await
      ImagePicker.launchImageLibraryAsync({
        mediaTypes: ImagePicker.MediaTypeOptions.Images,
        allowsEditing: true,
        aspect: [4, 3],
        quality: 0.1,
      });
```

```
    if (!imageFile.cancelled) {
        const file: any = imageFile.uri;
```

For React Native, use the following code:

```
const onImageUploadChange = async ():Promise<void> => {
    try {
        const options: ImageLibraryOptions = {
            mediaType: 'photo',
            quality: 0.1,
            maxWidth: 400,
            maxHeight: 300
        };

        launchImageLibrary(options,  async (response) => {
            console.log('Response = ', response);
            if (response.didCancel) {
                console.log('User cancelled image picker');
            } else if (response.errorCode) {
                console.log('ImagePicker Error: ',
                response.errorMessage);
            } else {
                setImg(response.uri as string);
                if (response.uri as string) {
                    const file: any = response.uri;
```

The second half of the method for the Expo and the React Native projects is the same; that is, calling the `urlToBlob` method that we created earlier to convert the URL into a blob in order to upload the user-selected image to Amplify Storage:

```
                const fileName: any = file.
                replace(/^.*[\\\/]/, '');
                const contentType: any =
                fileName.split('.').pop().toLowerCase();
                setInput("image", fileName);
                const responseData = await urlToBlob(file);

                Storage.put(fileName, responseData, {
                    contentType: 'image/' + contentType,
                })
```

```
                    .then(async (result: any) => {
                        console.log('result.key', result.key);
                        setImg((await Storage.get(result.key)) as
                        string);
                        console.log('onImageUploadChange
                        result:',
                        result);
                    })
                    .catch((err) => console.error(err));
                }
                console.log('onImageUploadChange img:', img);
            }
        });
    } catch (err) {
        console.error('onImageUploadChange err:', err);
    }
};
```

6. We will reuse the code from *Chapter 5*, *Creating a Blog Post with Amplify GraphQL*, on the GitHub repository to fetch the posts:

```
const fetchPosts = async (): Promise<any> => {
    try {
        console.log("fetching posts");
        const postData: any = await API.graphql(
            graphqlOperation(queries.listPosts)
        );
        const posts: any = postData.data.listPosts.items;
        setPosts(posts);
    } catch (err) {
        console.log("error fetching posts: ", err);
    }
};
```

7. We will use the `setInput` method to store the user input on the post state object in memory:

```
const setInput = (key: any, value: any): any => {
  setPostState({ ...postState, [key]: value });
};
```

8. We will need to update the `createPost` method in order to add the image key-value pair to the input object. This will allow us to store the unique image key in the database:

```
const createPost = async (): Promise<any> => {
  try {
    if (!postState.title || !postState.content) return;
    const post = { ...postState };
    console.log("creating post", post);
    const result = await API.graphql(
      graphqlOperation(mutations.createPost, {
        input: {
          title: post.title,
          content: post.content,
          image: post.image,
        },
      })
    );
    setPosts([...posts, post] as
    SetStateAction<never[]>);
    setPostState(defaultPostState);
    console.log("created post", result);
  } catch (err) {
    console.log("error creating post:", err);
  }
};
```

9. We don't need to change the `updatePost` method since users normally won't upload a new image to an old post. They will only update the content, so we can reuse the `updatePost` code from *Chapter 5, Creating a Blog Post with Amplify GraphQL*, here:

```
const updatePost = async (): Promise<any> => {
  try {
    if (!postState.title || !postState.content) return;
    const post = { ...postState };
    console.log("updating post", post);
    const result = await API.graphql(
      graphqlOperation(mutations.updatePost, {
        input: {
          id: post.id,
          title: post.title,
          content: post.content,
        },
      })
    );
    setUpdateSectionState(false);
    setCreateSectionState(true);
    console.log("updated post", result);
    setPostState(defaultPostState);
  } catch (err) {
    console.log("error updating post:", err);
  }
};
```

10. The same thing goes for the `deletePost` method – nothing needs to be changed here:

```
const deletePost = async (postID: string): Promise<any>
=> {
  try {
    if (!postID) return;
    console.log("deleting post", postID);
    const result = await API.graphql(
      graphqlOperation(mutations.deletePost, {
```

```
        input: {
            id: postID,
        },
    })
  );
  console.log("deleted post", result);
} catch (err) {
  console.log("error deleting post:", err);
  }
};
```

11. The same thing goes for the findPost method – nothing needs to be changed here either:

```
const findPosts = async (title: string): Promise<any>
=> {
  try {
    console.log("finding posts:", title);
    const postData: any = await API.graphql(
      graphqlOperation(queries.listPosts, {
        filter: {
          title: {
            contains: title,
          },
        },
      })
    );
    console.log("found posts:");
    const posts: any = postData.data.listPosts.items;
    setPosts(posts);
  } catch (err) {
    console.log("error finding posts ", err);
  }
};
```

12. In the `return` section, we only need to add the Amplify S3Image UI element to the code, along with its style. Make sure that you set the height and width to the S3Image object; otherwise, you won't be able to see the image. I spent almost an hour figuring that out since it's undocumented. We will reuse most of the code from *Chapter 5*, *Creating a Blog Post with Amplify GraphQL*, which you can find in this book's GitHub repository, such as the UI elements:

```
return (
    <SafeAreaView style={styles.safeArea}>
        <View style={styles.container}>
            <TextInput
                onChangeText={(val) => findPosts(val)}
                style={styles.input}
                placeholder="Search"
            />
```

13. `createSectionState` determines whether the create post UI or the update post UI will be shown to the user, depending on its state. This is based on user interaction:

```
{createSectionState ? (
    <View>
        <Text style={styles.title}>Create Post</Text>
        <View>
            <Text
                style={styles.button}
                onPress={() => {
                    onImageUploadChange();
                }}
            >
                Pick an image from camera roll
            </Text>
            {img ? (
                <Image
                    source={{ uri: img }}
                    style={{ width: 320, height: 200 }}
                />
            ) : null}
```

```
            </View>
            <TextInput
                onChangeText={ (val) => setInput ("title",
                val)}
                style={styles.input}
                value={postState.title}
                placeholder="Title"
            />
```

14. Display the value of the `postState` object in the UI to show what the user has entered, such as the content of the post:

```
            <TextInput
                onChangeText={ (val) => setInput ("content",
                val)}
                style={styles.textArea}
                value={postState.content}
                placeholder="Content"
            />
            <Text style={styles.button}
            onPress={createPost}>
                Create Post
            </Text>
        </View>
    ) : null}
```

15. The `updateSectionState` section will be the same as the one provided in the GitHub repository for *Chapter 5, Creating a Blog Post with Amplify GraphQL*, so we will reuse that code here:

```
        {updateSectionState ? (
            <View>
                <Text style={styles.title}>Update Post</Text>
                <TextInput
                    onChangeText={ (val) => setInput ("title",
                    val)}
                    style={styles.input}
                    value={postState.title}
                    placeholder="Title"
```

```
        />
        <TextInput
            onChangeText={(val) => setInput("content",
            val)}
            style={styles.textArea}
            value={postState.content}
            placeholder="Content"
        />
        <Text style={styles.button}
        onPress={updatePost}>
            Update Post
        </Text>
    </View>
) : null}
```

16. The only changes we will make to the `return` section will be done in this step. We only need to add the Amplify S3Image UI element to display the images that are fetched from the database. Remember to set the style alongside the width and height; otherwise, we won't be able to see it:

```
<ScrollView style={styles.scrollView}>
    {posts.map((post: any, index: any) => (
        <View key={post.id ? post.id : index}
        style={styles.post}>
            <S3Image style={styles.postImage}
            level="public"
            imgKey={post.image} />
```

17. The remaining code will be the same as the code in *Chapter 5*, *Creating a Blog Post with Amplify GraphQL*. Make sure that you save the file once you've finished editing the `App.tsx` file:

```
            <Text style={styles.postTitle}>
                {post.title}
            </Text>
            <Text style={styles.postContent}>
            {post.content}</Text>
            <View style={{ flexDirection: "row" }}>
                <Text
```

```
                    style={styles.postUpdate}
                    onPress={() => {
                        setPostState(post);
                        setUpdateSectionState(true);
                        setCreateSectionState(false);
                    }}
                > Update </Text>
                <Text
                    style={styles.postDelete}
                    onPress={() => {
                        deletePost(post.id);
                    }}
                >
                    Delete
                </Text>
              </View>
            </View>
          ))}
        </ScrollView>
        <StatusBar style="auto" />
      </View>
    </SafeAreaView>
  );
};
export default App;
```

18. Let's open the `AppStyles.ts` file and add the following code anywhere before the closing tag. This will set the image style with a fixed width and height:

> **Important note**
> If you don't set these values, the image won't be display on screen.

```
import {StyleSheet} from 'react-native';

export default StyleSheet.create({
  safeArea: {
    flex: 1,
```

```
      marginHorizontal: 16,
    },
  container: {flex: 1, justifyContent: 'flex-start',
  padding:
  30},
  title: {fontSize: 22, fontWeight: 'bold', marginBottom:
  10},
  input: {height: 50, backgroundColor: '#ddd',
  marginBottom:
  10, padding: 10},
  textArea: {
    backgroundColor: '#ddd',
    padding: 10,
    height: 70,
    marginBottom: 10,
  },
  button: {
    backgroundColor: 'red',
    color: 'white',
    fontWeight: 'bold',
    padding: 10,
    textAlign: 'center',
    fontSize: 15,
  },
  scrollView: {
    marginTop: 20,
  },
  post: {marginBottom: 15},
```

Here is where we might want to add the code to set the height and width values for the S3Image component:

```
  postImage: { height: 300, width: 400 },
  postTitle: {fontSize: 18, fontWeight: 'bold'},
  postContent: {fontSize: 16, marginBottom: 10},
  postUpdate: {fontSize: 12, width: '50%', textAlign:
  'center'},
```

```
postDelete: {fontSize: 12, width: '50%', textAlign:
'center'},
});
```

19. Run the `yarn ios` command or the `yarn android` command to compile the app to check if it works.

    You should be able to see the app running on the iOS 14 simulator with the desired iOS device, such as the latest iPhone 12 Pro Max, as follows:

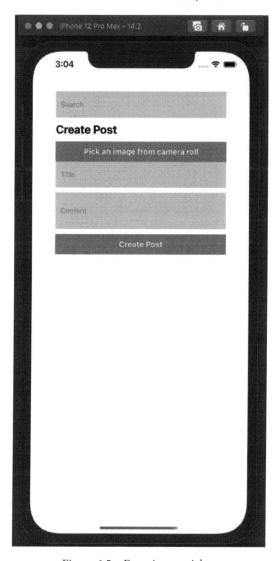

Figure 6.5 – Expo image picker

You can always switch to other devices to see if the design aligns properly with different screen sizes.

20. Click on the **Pick an image from camera roll** button and choose an image to upload from the camera roll:

Figure 6.6 – Expo image gallery

Since we have set the canvas to 4:3, you can crop the selected image with the 4:3 aspect ratio. If your design preference is 16:9, you can always change the aspect ratio to 16:9, as well as the width and height of the Amplify S3Image UI element:

Figure 6.7 – Expo image cropping

Once you've done this, the image will be uploaded to the S3 Bucket automatically and return the unique identifier of the image. You can use this image to retrieve it from the S3 Bucket, as we discussed in the code:

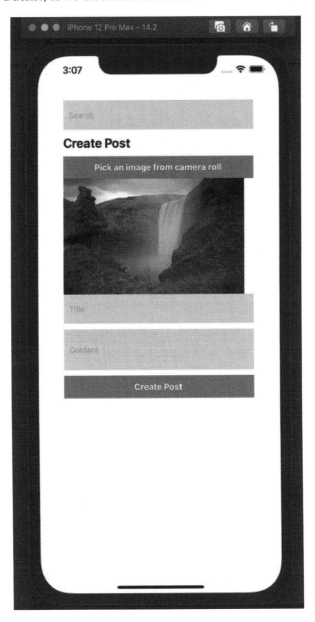

Figure 6.8 – S3Image uploaded with Expo

It's just that simple. With a few lines of code, you can upload and retrieve the image between the user's device and the AWS cloud. Thankfully, the AWS Amplify solution does all the heavy lifting behind the scenes. In the next section, we will learn how to create and retrieve the blog post, along with the images, in real time with Expo and React Native.

> **Important note**
>
> If you are not sure what your editor is asking you to do, you may wish to communicate through other methods, such as a messaging service or a telephone call. This is allowed, but please bear in mind that scheduling may be an issue! Your editor may be based in a different time zone from you, and their office hours may not align with your hours of availability.

Listing all the blog posts with real-time updates with React Native and Expo

In this section, we will learn how to add a real-time subscription to the app, which is important if you are creating an app where you want to let users subscribe to any updates that they are interested in, such as receiving a notification about a blog post or a new article for a website or app. Let's get started:

1. Open the App.tsx file again and add the following code anywhere within the main App function code block:

```
const createSubscription: any = API.graphql(
  graphqlOperation(subscriptions.onCreatePost)
);
createSubscription.subscribe({
  next: (postData: any) => {
    console.log("onCreatePost", postData);
    fetchPosts();
  },
});
const updateSubscription: any = API.graphql(
  graphqlOperation(subscriptions.onUpdatePost)
);
updateSubscription.subscribe({
  next: (postData: any) => {
    console.log("onUpdatePost", postData);
```

```
        fetchPosts();
    },
  });
  const deleteSubscription: any = API.graphql(
    graphqlOperation(subscriptions.onDeletePost)
  );
  DeleteSubscription .subscribe({
    next: (postData: any) => {
      console.log("onDeletePost", postData);
      fetchPosts();
    },
  });
```

2. Once you've done this, save the App.tsx file and run the yarn ios or yarn android command to see if the app works.

3. Let's choose a different photo this time and create a proper blog post by giving it a title and some content. Then, press the **Create Post** button:

Figure 6.9 – Creating a new post with the Expo image picker

You should be able to see the app being updated instantly with the blog post, just below the **Create Post** section:

Figure 6.10 – Real-time update with a subscription

You can scroll through the posts if you have created a lot of posts

Real-time subscriptions can be very useful in apps, especially if you want to engage your users more frequently by updating the app's content in real time. AWS Amplify has done an enormous amount of work simplifying all the real-time interaction for developers, which makes it easier to build new apps with new features.

Summary

In this chapter, we have learned how to create an image blog post with real-time subscriptions for both web apps and mobile apps with React, Expo, and React Native. We also learned how to add the pre-built Photo Picker component from the Amplify library to the app, how to create a feature for uploading the photo to Amplify Storage, and how to list all the blog posts for the users in real time. These features allow modern websites and apps to update without the user having to either refresh their website manually or pull to refresh their app on their smart phone. This improves the user experience in general. The code bases between ReactJS, React Native, and Expo are very similar, which means you can share most of the code between these projects and reuse it.

In the next chapter, we will learn how to create an Amplify DevOps pipeline, which can deploy the ReactJS code to Amplify Hosting automatically, whenever we submit new code to the repository.

Section 3: Production Readiness

You might want to tell the world that you have created a photo sharing app on social media, and for this, you will need to make sure it is production-ready. For instance, by adding a custom domain name, a DevOps pipeline, and end-to-end test automation, if you want to add more features to the app later.

In this section, there are the following chapters:

- *Chapter 7, Setting Up an Amplify Pipeline*
- *Chapter 8, Test Automation with Cypress*
- *Chapter 9, Setting Up a Custom Domain Name and the Amplify Admin UI*

7
Setting Up an Amplify Pipeline

So far, we have made some significant progress with AWS Amplify. In this chapter, we will learn how to apply DevOps and even NoOps with the Amplify pipeline. DevOps or NoOps can help your development team deliver new features to production very quickly.

Some people would call DevOps a culture, a practice, an approach, a framework, or even a set of tools. Well, the fact is that all these names are correct and do not contradict each other. Because Devs and Ops are working more closely than ever before, there is definitely a culture change, especially with the AWS Amplify pipeline. It is a good practice to shorten the cycle time from build, test, and deployment to production. It is a better approach compared to manual deployment. It is a toolchain that helps you apply continuous integration, test automation, and deployment as easily as pushing a button. If you are using the Amplify pipeline, you might not even need to worry about Ops anymore, because this has been handled by the Amplify pipeline itself; you only need to set up the YAML file and the pipeline will be ready to go. Therefore, if you use the Amplify pipeline for your new or existing projects, you are basically skipping the DevOps era and jumping right into the NoOps era.

In this chapter, we will learn how to set up the AWS Amplify pipeline with just a few lines of code. We will be covering the following topics:

- Enabling the DevOps pipeline

- Adding the YAML file

- Email notifications

- Troubleshooting techniques

- Triggering the pipeline

Building a new product has never been easier. With Amplify, you can put more focus on enhancing and enriching the user experience instead of fiddling around with infrastructure and operations by adopting the cloud-native DevOps pipeline.

Technical requirements

This chapter requires you to complete the exercises in *Chapter 1, Getting Familiar with the Amplify CLI and Amplify Console*, to ensure you have added **Amplify Hosting** to your project. Amplify Hosting only works with the ReactJS and React Native for Web projects. Yes, React Native for Web is a thing in 2021 since the React community has been working on it for a few years; it is in its beta stage at the moment, which is very stable. React Native for Web can be enabled for both Expo and React Native apps. Many well-known companies are using React Native for Web in production, including Twitter, Flipkart, Uber, and The Times.

If your app is based on Expo, then React Native for Web should already be part of the package as Expo SDK version 33, called the Expo Web. However, if your app is based on React Native, then you will need to run the following command to add the React Native for Web library to your project:

```
yarn add react-native-web
```

You can download the file from the following link: `https://github.com/PacktPublishing/Rapid-Application-Development-with-AWS-Amplify/tree/master/ch7`.

Enabling the Amplify DevOps pipeline

To enable the Amplify DevOps pipeline, the app must be set up for continuous deployment and connected to a GitHub repository. Follow these steps to enable the continuous deployment pipeline for your apps:

1. Open a Terminal and enter the `amplify add hosting` command for the ReactJS, React Native for Web, and Expo Web projects. Then, select `Continuous deployment` as `type`. This will open Amplify Console in your browser:

```
amplify add hosting

? Select the plugin module to execute Hosting with
Amplify Console (Managed hosting with custom domains,
Continuous deployment)

? Choose a type Continuous deployment (Git-based
deployments)

? Continuous deployment is configured in the Amplify
Console. Please hit enter once you connect your
repository
```

2. Choose your favorite GitHub repository provider and click **Connect branch**:

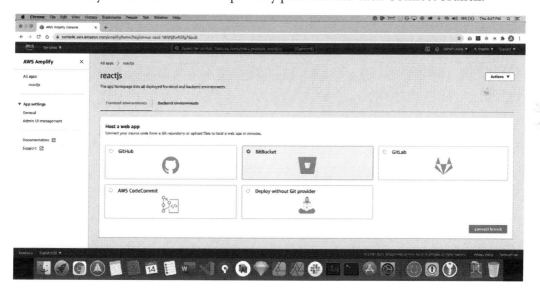

Figure 7.1 – Connecting to a GitHub repository

3. Click on the drop - down menu to select the correct repository for your app and select the branch to connect to.

4. If your app is a monorepo, which means it contains a lot of subfolders that contain different apps within one single repository, then you can check the **Connecting a monorepo? Pick a folder** checkbox to enable the options in *step 4*. Otherwise, simply click **Next** and skip *step 4*:

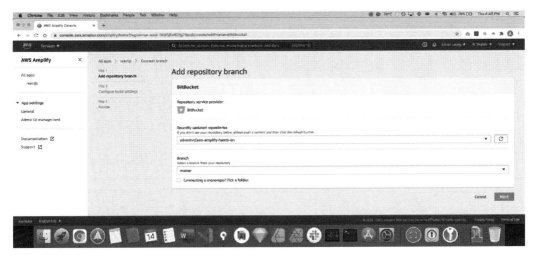

Figure 7.2 – Selecting a repository and a branch to connect to

5. Enter the folder path, as shown in the following screenshot, if your repository is a monorepo and click **Next**:

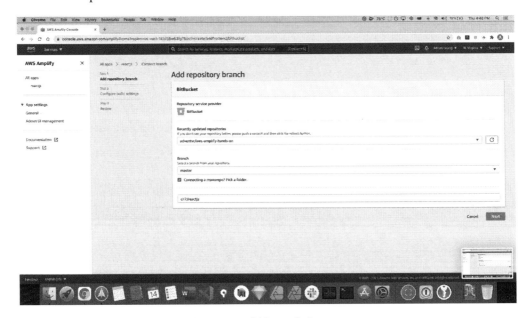

Figure 7.3 – Entering a folder path for your monorepo

The app name will be generated based on the app name that you defined previously or the monorepo path name, which depends on the previous step. Amplify Console will detect the frameworks and build settings based on your project. In this example, the Amplify pipeline detected the React frontend and Amplify backend frameworks and then generated the **Build and test** settings as a YAML file, which you can download to your project. You can click on **Download** to modify the YAML file offline and store it in the root folder of your project repository, or click **Edit** and edit it online:

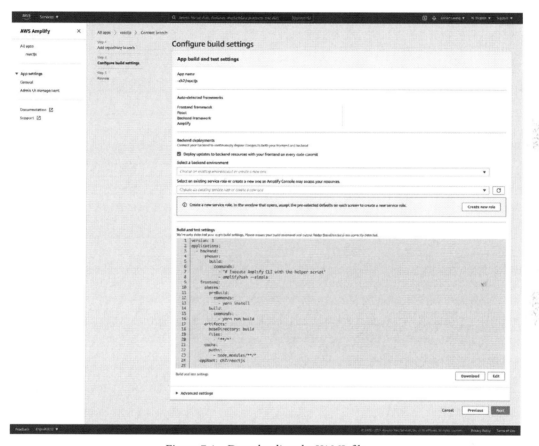

Figure 7.4 – Downloading the YAML file

6. **For advanced users only**: If you have your own Docker image that contains
    more specific frameworks and a Linux OS that you prefer, then you can click on
    the **Advanced settings** options and specify the Docker repository in the **Build
    image** section:

▼ **Advanced settings**

Build image
Use our default build container, or provide your own. **Learn more**

    Reference your build image (E.g. <docker repository>/<docker image name>)

Environment variables
Add environment variables to save secrets and API keys that you do not want to store in your repository

Key	Value	
USER_BRANCH	dev	**Remove**

Add

Jekyll
Hugo
Yarn
Bundler
Cypress
VuePress
Gatsby CLI

Add package version override ▲

Live package updates
Override the default installed versions of packages or tools for your app.

Package	Version	
Amplify CLI	latest	**Remove**

Figure 7.5 – Advanced settings page

You can also add environment variables in order to save secrets and API keys
instead of hardcoding them in your code, which is very handy.

Since we created the backend environment and backend role in the previous
chapter, we can simply choose the backend environment and the backend role from
the dropdowns. We can leave the **Deploy updates to backend resources with your
frontend on evert code commit** checkbox option checked if we want the pipeline
to build both the frontend and backend code on every commit, which is very useful
for new projects:

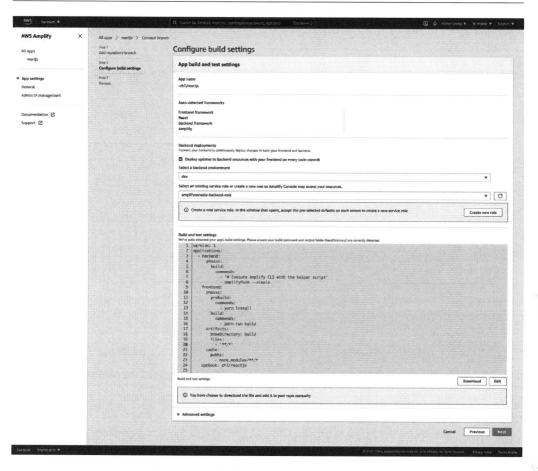

Figure 7.6 – Clicking Next to review the settings

7.   Click **Next** when you are ready.

8. Double-check the build pipeline settings and click **Save and deploy** when you are ready:

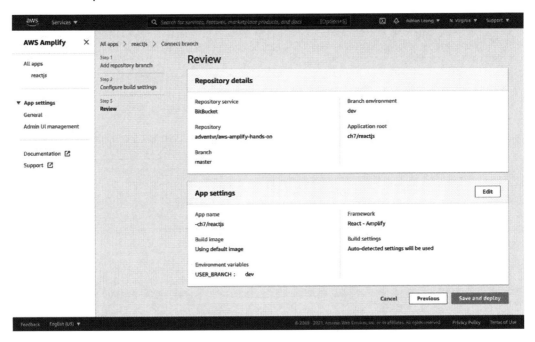

Figure 7.7 – Reviewing the settings

9. You will see the **Creating branch: master success** message or a similar successful alert, as follows:

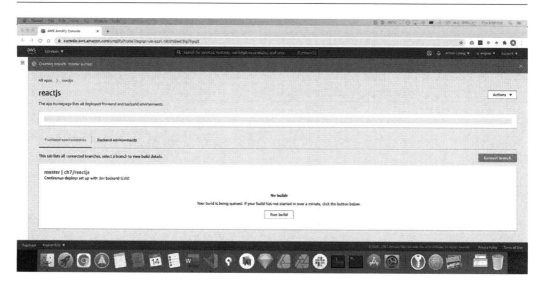

Figure 7.8 – Connected to a repository successfully

10. After a few seconds, the pipeline will pick up the code from the repository and start building the environment automatically. It will go through the entire DevOps pipeline, which will take around 4 minutes to complete for our first build. When the build is successful, you will see that the entire pipeline is green for all the stages; that is, **Provision**, **Build**, **Deploy**, and **Verify**:

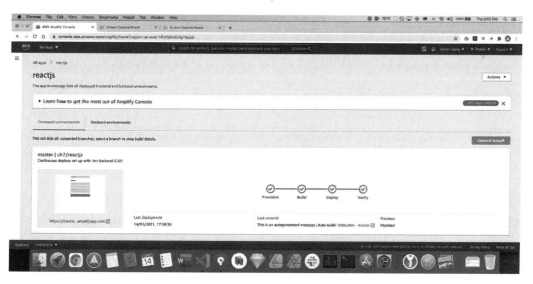

Figure 7.9 – Checking out the new build

You can click on the newly generated URL to check out the deployment with Amplify Hosting.

If you click on the **Verify** option, you should be able to see how the app is being rendered on different screen sizes, as follows:

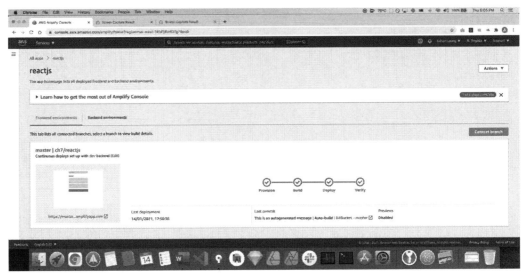

Figure 7.10 – Verifying the new build – part I

As you can see, the ReactJS app is being rendered between my iPad and smartphone, which is very useful for fixing any cosmetic frontend alignment and padding issues on different screen sizes:

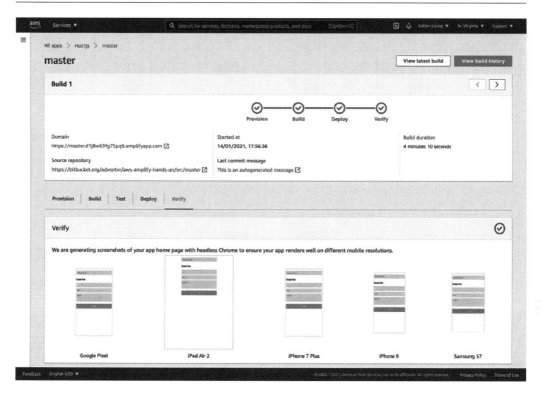

Figure 7.11 – Verifying the new build – part II

A designer and a developer can work very closely to discuss how the app should be rendered between big and small screen sizes. They won't need to buy all the devices and test them offline, which is a massive time saver.

11. Now, go back to the Terminal and hit *Enter* once you are done. You will see that a new URL has been generated, as follows:

```
Amplify hosting urls:
https://master.xxxxxxxxx.amplifyapp.com
```

In this section, we learned how to enable the DevOps pipeline by adding Amplify Hosting, adding continuous deployment, and deploying the web app to a URL. For this, we had to perform a one-time setup; now, all subsequent deployments to the environment will be done automatically. This is the power of continuous deployment through the Amplify DevOps pipeline. We should call it NoOps instead of DevOps because all the Ops has been handled by the DevOps pipeline itself. Now that we've configured it properly, we can forget about it for all subsequent code commits to the GitHub repository. This is the power of **Continuous Integration and Continuous Deployment (CI/CD)** with both the frontend and backend. In the next section, we will learn how to add the YAML file manually to the DevOps pipeline.

Adding the YAML file

In the previous section, we downloaded the YAML template that was generated by Amplify Console, which was based on the auto detection of our technology stacks. However, as we already know, sometimes, we might need to tweak it a little to fulfil the requirements of the project.

Open the DevOps Pipeline YAML file that we downloaded earlier. The build steps are very straightforward. The file installs the libraries for both the backend and the frontend and then caches all the node modules that have been installed:

```yaml
version: 1
applications:
  - backend:
      phases:
        build:
          commands:
            - '# Execute Amplify CLI with the helper script'
            - amplifyPush --simple
    frontend:
      phases:
        preBuild:
          commands:
            - yarn install
        build:
          commands:
            - yarn run build
```

```
    artifacts:
        baseDirectory: build
        files:
            - '**/*'
    cache:
        paths:
            - node_modules/**/*
    appRoot: ch7/reactjs
```

If you're wondering which Node.js version has been used for the build, perhaps because your app's build failed due to the wrong Node.js version being used, you can click on the **Provision** button link to find out more information from the provision log:

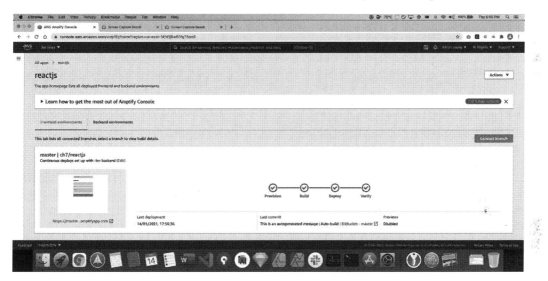

Figure 7.12 – Provision

You can find out about the versions of the frameworks and Docker image information from the provision log. As shown in the following screenshot, the default Node.js version has been set to 12:

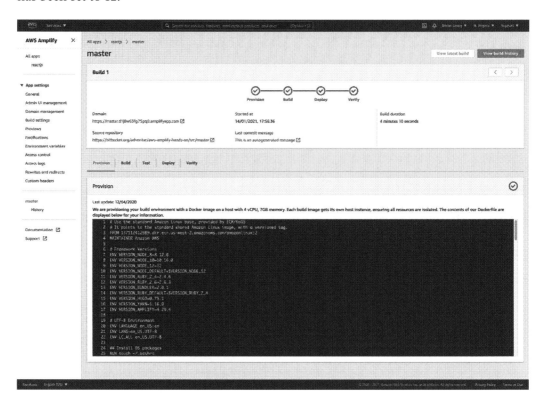

Figure 7.13 – Provision log

Let's edit the YML file and specify the Node version as 12 with `nvm use $VERSION_NODE_12` if we want to specify the version of Node.js. But if your app is based on v8 or v10, you can simply change the node version to `nvm use $VERSION_NODE_8` or `nvm use $VERSION_NODE_10`, respectively. We can specify the build artifacts of the frontend in the build folder by recommitting the code to the repository:

```
version: 2
backend:
  phases:
    preBuild:
      commands:
        - nvm use $VERSION_NODE_12
```

```yaml
      - amplifyPush --simple
  build:
    commands:
      - nvm use $VERSION_NODE_12
      - yarn install
frontend:
  phases:
    preBuild:
      commands:
        - nvm use $VERSION_NODE_12
        - yarn install
    build:
      commands:
        - nvm use $VERSION_NODE_12
        - yarn build
  artifacts:
    baseDirectory: build
    files:
      - '**/*'
  cache:
    paths:
      - node_modules/**/*
```

As soon as you've committed the code to the GitHub repository, you should see that the Amplify pipeline is trigged automatically on the web portal:

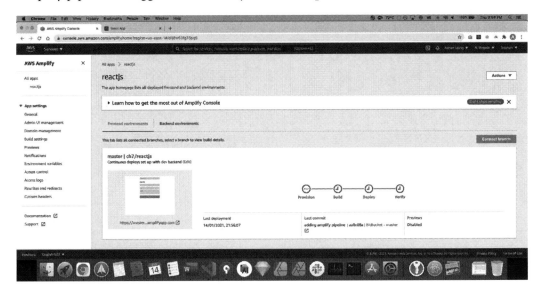

Figure 7.14 – Auto build

The commands inside the YML file are the same commands that you entered in the Terminal. This means that you can enter some specific Linux command there to perform specific tasks, such as installing some SDKs, downloading some files, uploading artifices to somewhere else, and more. There is no limit of what you can do with the DevOps pipeline. In the next section, we will learn how to enable email notifications for the build status.

Enabling email notifications

The Amplify pipeline is very handy for CI/CD, but what if the build time is getting longer due to our application getting bigger? We don't want to sit and wait for the build result to come back while working on other tasks during the build. How can we get notified when a build has finished, regardless of whether it's failed or been successful? The Amplify pipeline can do this for us. All we need to do is go to the **Notification** section of Amplify Console and add our email address there so that we get a notification. To enable email notifications, follow these steps:

1. Click on the **Add notification** button or **Manage notifications**:

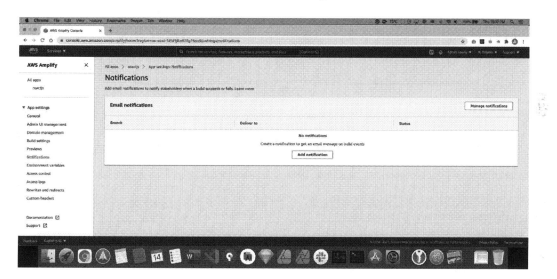

Figure 7.15 – Email notifications

After clicking on **Manage notifications** or the **Add notification** button, you will see the text field for the email address and a drop - down menu for the branches. You can add more than one email address by clicking the **Add Email** button for more input fields.

2. Enter the email addresses that you want to receive notifications about the build succeeding or failing.

3. Select a specific branch of the repository via the dropdown for each email address.

   If you haven't created any other branch yet, then you can choose **master** for now or **All Branches** if you want to be notified of all the builds from all the branches. For trunk-based development workflows, which means there's no repository branching, we should choose **master**, but for feature branch development workflows, where you can create a branch for each feature, we might want to choose **All Branches** instead.

4. Click on **Save** when you are ready:

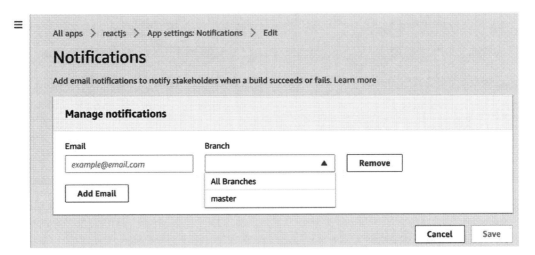

Figure 7.16 – Adding emails for notifications

> **Important note**
> If you don't want to receive millions of build notifications through emails, you can opt for some modern communication tools such as Slack instead for some ChatOps.

You can create an incoming webhook (please check out the *Enable webhooks* documentation for further instructions at `https://api.slack.com/messaging/webhooks#enable_webhooks`) and then call the webhook through the YAML file. You can call the same webhook multiple times in different build stages with different messages with emojis for a better experience, as shown here:

```
version: 2.1
backend:
  phases:
```

```
  build:
    commands:
      - curl -X POST --data-urlencode 'payload={"text":"Build
      started, hold my 🍺…"}' https://hooks.slack.com/
      services/xxxxx/xxxxx/xxxxxxxxxxxx
      - nvm use $VERSION_NODE_12
      - '# Execute Amplify CLI with the helper script'
      - amplifyPush --simple
frontend:
  phases:
    preBuild:
      commands:
        - yarn install
    build:
      commands:
        - yarn run build
        - curl -X POST --data-urlencode
        'payload={"text":"Build
        finished, where is my 🍺…"}' https://hooks.slack.
        com/
        services/xxxxx/xxxxx/xxxxxxxxxxxx
  artifacts:
    baseDirectory: build
    files:
      - '**/*'
  cache:
    paths:
      - node_modules/**/*
appRoot: ch7/reactjs
```

You can always set up a test version of the web app with a feature branch if you prefer feature-based development (that is, feature-driven development with multiple feature branches) over trunk-based development (master branch only). You can go through the connect branch process again for the additional branches on the app page of Amplify Console. In the next section, we will learn how to troubleshoot if the build goes wrong and we receive a build failure notification.

Troubleshooting techniques

You might be wondering how we are going to find out what happens when the build fails or what happens if the build doesn't work anymore due to library upgrades. So, in this section, we will learn how to look at the online console logs to find out about what went wrong. Let's get started:

1. Let's create a failed build scenario by adding a bug to one of our React apps. To do this, comment out one of the `import` statements in the `App.tsx` file and recommit the code to the repository after:

```
import * as subscriptions from "./graphql/subscriptions";
// import { AmplifyS3Image } from "@aws-amplify/
ui-react";
import awsExports from "./aws-exports";
```

2. Now, go to Amplify Console to check out the new build. The build should have failed due to the error that we created within the app.

3. Click on the **Build** tab of the DevOps pipeline and expand the collapsible area where the frontend error occurred to check out the console log, as follows:

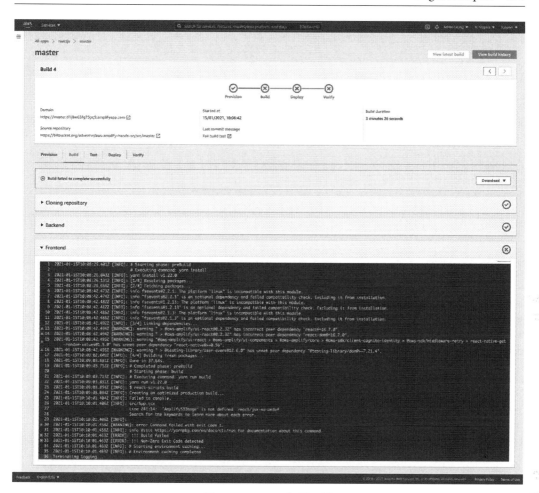

Figure 7.17 – Failed build

As we can see, the error was caused by the app because it failed to compile due to the missing library import. The error looks something like this:

```
[INFO]: Failed to compile.
[INFO]: src/App.tsx
        Line 241:14:   'AmplifyS3Image' is not defined
        react/jsx-no-undef
        Search for the keywords to learn more about each
        error.
[WARNING]: error Command failed with exit code 1.
[INFO]: info Visit https://yarnpkg.com/en/docs/cli/run
for documentation about this command.
```

```
[ERROR]: !!! Build failed
[ERROR]: !!! Non-Zero Exit Code detected
[INFO]: # Starting environment caching...
[INFO]: # Environment caching completed
```

If we run the `yarn start` command in the Terminal of the web app, we will see the following error on the browser:

Failed to compile

```
src/App.tsx
  Line 241:14:  'AmplifyS3Image' is not defined  react/jsx-no-undef

Search for the keywords to learn more about each error.
```

This error occurred during the build time and cannot be dismissed.

Figure 7.18 – Error message on the browser

Therefore, if the frontend and backend have a compilation time error, the DevOps pipeline will pick up this error and stop deploying the artifact to the environment. If we set up email notification settings, then we should receive an email about the build failing so that we can continue working on other tasks while waiting for the build to be completed.

The DevOps pipeline is very useful for developers and the development team for finding errors during integration. That's why it's also called the CI/CD pipeline, also known as Continuous Integration and Continuous Delivery or Continuous Deployment. If the targeted environment is the production environment, then we should use the term Continuous Deployment; otherwise, we should use the term Continuous Delivery. Continuous Integration happens when we deploy both the frontend and backend artifacts to the environment and perform an end-to-end test, which ensures that both the frontend and backend have been integrated successfully.

Important note

If your app is a **Progressive Web App** (**PWA**), you might want to enable performance mode to invalidate the **Content Delivery Network** (**CDN**) cache on every commit instantly via instant deployment. Otherwise, the web browser on the client side will cache the previous frontend PWA deployment. You can find the settings by going to **Amplify Console | Your Web App | App Settings | General | Branch Actions dropdown | Enable performance mode** to enable this, as follows:

Branch auto-disconnection
Automatically disconnect branches in Amplify Console when deleting a branch in your source repository

◯ Disabled

| | | | Disconnect branch |
| Disable auto build |
| Enable performance mode |

Branches

| | Action ▲ | Connect a branch |

	Branch name	URL prefix	Auto-build Info	Performance mode Info
◉	master	master	Enabled	Disabled

Figure 7.19 – Performance mode

In this section, we learned about various troubleshooting techniques, such as where to find the error logs to pinpoint errors. In the next section, we will show you a few ways to trigger the Amplify build pipeline.

Triggering the pipeline

There are a few ways to trigger the DevOps pipeline. We can trigger the pipeline by committing the code through the repository and triggering the build automatically, or by directly triggering the pipeline manually.

Imagine working with multiple team members who are working on the trunk together and we keep triggering the pipeline with an unfinished feature. Ideally, we would like to trigger the pipeline when the team is ready to integrate. To do this, we will need to disable the auto build feature of the pipeline:

1.   Go to **Amplify Console | App | General | Branches**, click on the **Action** dropdown, and select the **Disable auto build** option:

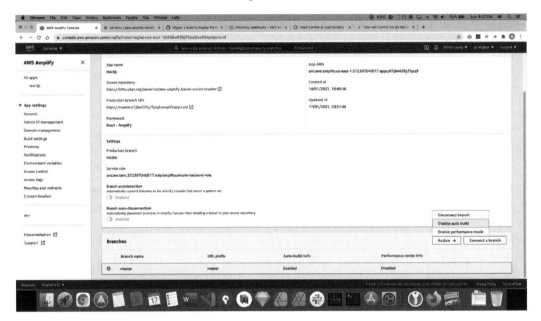

Figure 7.20 – Disable auto build option

After this, we will need to create a webhook on the **Build Settings** page.

2. Click on the **Create webhook** button:

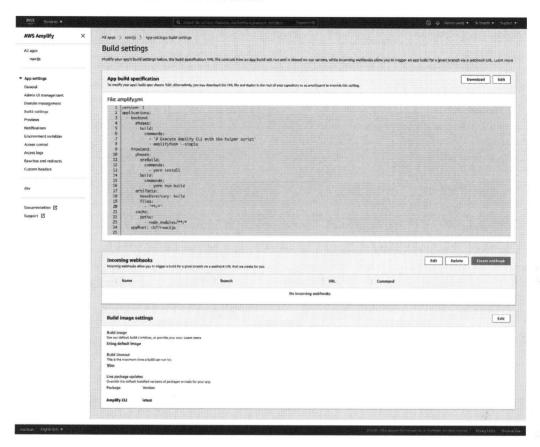

Figure 7.21 – Create webhook button

3. Enter a desired name for the webhook or leave it blank. If you leave it blank, a default name will be used instead; that is, `triggermaster`. Once you've done this, select a branch to build. Then, click the **Save** button:

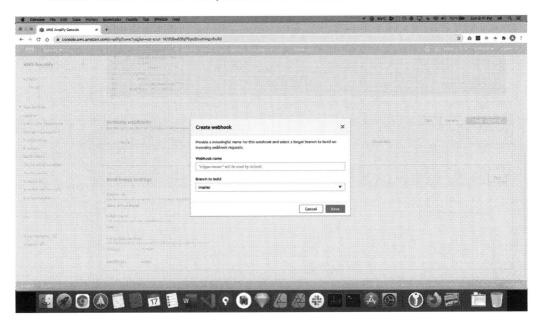

Figure 7.22 – Creating the webhook

4. Now, copy the newly created webhook URL by clicking the **copy icon** button under the **Command** section:

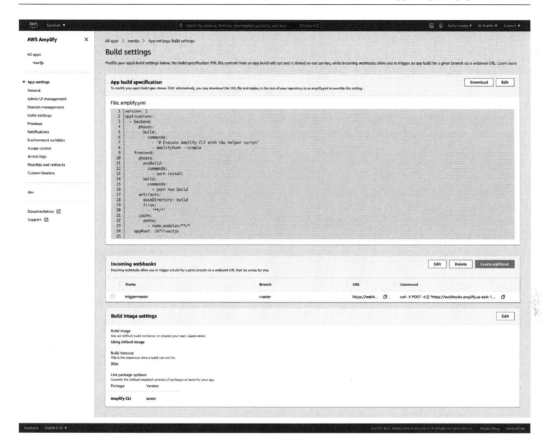

Figure 7.23 – Copying the webhook

5. Next, we will edit the App.tsx file of the app again and revert the changes we've made by uncommenting the import, as follows:

```
import * as subscriptions from "./graphql/subscriptions";
import { AmplifyS3Image } from "@aws-amplify/ui-react";
import awsExports from "./aws-exports";
```

6. Recommit the code to the repository. You will notice that the pipeline has not been triggered yet because we have disabled auto build. Now, run the webhook that was copied in *step 4* in the Terminal and hit *Enter*:

```
curl -X POST -d {} "https://webhooks.amplify.us-east-1.
amazonaws.com/prod/webhooks?id=xxxxx-xxxx-xxxx-xxxx-xxxxx
xxxxx&token=xxxxxxxxxx&operation=startbuild" -H "Content-
Type:application/json"
```

We should get a response message back from the webhook in the Terminal, as follows:

```
{"SendMessageResponse":{"ResponseMetadata":{"Reques
tId":"xxxxx-xxxx-xxxx-xxxx-xxxxxxxxxx"},"SendMessage
Result":{"MD5OfMessageAttributes":"xxxxxxxxxx","MD5O
fMessageBody":"xxxxxxxxxx","MD5OfMessageSystemAtt
ributes":null,"MessageId":"xxxxx-xxxx-xxxx-xxxx-
xxxxxxxxxx","SequenceNumber":null}}}%
```

7. Go back to Amplify Console. You will see that the build pipeline has been triggered successfully:

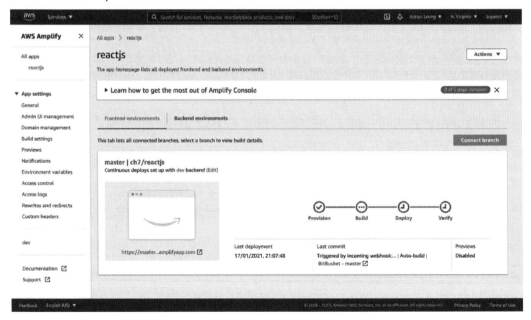

Figure 7.24 – Triggering the build with a webhook

Remember that the incoming webhook only supports the HEAD commit at this stage and not the commit ID. Therefore, we cannot trigger the previous build successfully just yet.

The incoming webhook can be very useful as we can automate the workflow, such as by setting up nightly builds and before-the-end of-the-day build activities for the team so that they can find bugs that need to be fixed, which is the true DevOps culture. We shouldn't let bugs pile up; instead, we should fix them as soon as we can. For some development teams that like challenges, I would recommend trying trunk-based development to encourage continuous integration, which happens with any code that is committed by development team members. This way, the team can see the benefit of using the build pipeline because if the integration process goes wrong, the problem can be fixed immediately to help us avoid technical debt.

Summary

In this chapter, we learned how to set up the Amplify DevOps pipeline, which automates the entire build workflow. We looked at various ways of sending notifications about when the build succeeded or failed. After that, we discussed some different ways of triggering the build and how it works in different kinds of branching scenarios.

Finally, we saw what NoOps (or LessOps) is all about. As we already know, DevOps exists for microservices or monolith architectures, but NoOps should be used for serverless technologies such as AWS Amplify Function or a **Function as a Service (FaaS)** such as Lambda. This is because we don't really need to set up nor maintain the infrastructure for the CI/CD pipeline.

In the next chapter, we will be learning about end-to-end test automation. I can say that this is a huge time saver based on my experience with many development teams that build enterprise solutions.

8
Test Automation with Cypress

In this chapter, we will learn how to add test automation to our Amplify apps with Cypress. The AWS Amplify team announced that they added the test phase to the build pipeline of Cypress in late 2019, which set themselves apart from the competition. Many might argue that **end-to-end (e2e)** test automation requires a lot of effort to maintain, but e2e test automation has actually become much easier to implement than ever before.

Before we talk about end-to-end test automation, we should talk about **Behavior-Driven Development (BDD)**. BDD is a way to shorten the feedback loop for the development cycle with e2e test automation. BDD is also known as **Specification by Example** and **Executable Specification**. Earlier in this book, we had to write specification documentation for the development team to write code and then let the testing team test the system manually. This may still sound familiar to many companies. But in the last 10 years, technology has evolved rapidly, so we should adopt a better development workflow to shorten the lead time.

In this chapter, we will cover the following topics so that we can practice BDD first-hand:

- Setting up Cypress with Cucumber
- Understanding the workflow to leverage BDD
- Writing executable User Stories in Gherkin

- Writing test cases as step definitions with TypeScript
- Integrating Cypress with the DevOps pipeline

By the end of this chapter, you should have a good understanding of the true beauty of agile development with BDD and e2e test automation. This improves the quality and reduce the rework rate significantly.

Technical requirements

To carry out the exercises in this chapter, you must have completed the exercises in the previous chapters so that you can apply end-to-end test automation to the web app. Cypress will only work for web technologies such as ReactJS, so if your app is based on React Native, you will have to add the `react-native-web` library to the project to make it work. However, for the React Expo app, which already has the Expo Web library built into it, you don't need to do anything.

You can download the files for this chapter from the following link: `https://github.com/PacktPublishing/Rapid-Application-Development-with-AWS-Amplify/tree/master/ch8/reactjs`.

Setting up Cypress with Cucumber

Let's open the project again and run the following command in the Terminal to install the libraries for BDD:

```
yarn add -D cypress cypress-cucumber-preprocessor @cypress/
webpack-preprocessor @types/cypress-cucumber-preprocessor
mochawesome mochawesome-report mochawesome-merge mochawesome-
report-generator ts-loader
```

Here, we have added the Cypress and Cucumber libraries for BDD, as well as the related Mocha awesome library for generating test reports that the Amplify pipeline can pick up.

Before we start integrating Cypress and Cucumber, we should initialize Cypress in our project so that Cypress can generate everything that's necessary for integration:

1. Run the following command in the Terminal to initiate Cypress in our project:

   ```
   yarn run cypress open
   ```

2. The Cypress binary should launch the very first time and generate the necessary files, as follows:

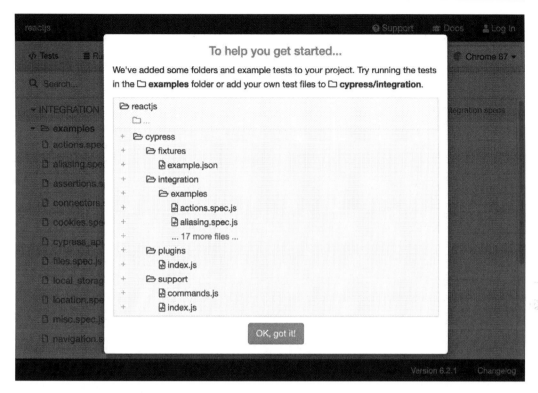

Figure 8.1 – Cypress initialization

3. Open the cypress.json file and add the following code to set up the mochaawesome report:

```
{
    "reporter": "mochawesome",
    "reporterOptions": {
        "reportDir": "cypress/report/mochawesome-report/",
        "overwrite": false,
        "html": false,
        "json": true,
        "timestamp": "mmddyyyy_HHMMss"
    },
    "baseUrl": "http://localhost:3000",
    "chromeWebSecurity": false,
    "defaultCommandTimeout": 120000,
    "execTimeout": 120000,
    "taskTimeout": 120000,
```

```
    "pageLoadTimeout": 120000,
    "requestTimeout": 120000,
    "responseTimeout": 120000,
    "screenshotsFolder": "cypress/report/screenshots",
    "videosFolder": "cypress/report/videos"
}
```

4. Create a file called cypress.js in the root directory of the app folder with the following code. This will configure Cypress and help merge multiple reports from different executable specifications into one big report as Living Documentation:

```
const marge = require('mochawesome-report-generator')
const { merge } = require('mochawesome-merge')
const reports = { reportDir: 'mochawesome-report' }
const mergedReport = { reportDir: 'cypress/report/
mochawesome-report' }
merge(reports).then((report) => marge.create(report,
mergedReport))
```

5. Create a file called tsconfig.json under the cypress folder that contains the following code to enable TypeScript for Cypress:

```
{
    "compilerOptions": {
        "target": "esnext",
        "types": ["cypress"],
        "lib": ["dom", "dom.iterable", "esnext"],
        "allowJs": true,
        "skipLibCheck": true,
        "esModuleInterop": true,
        "allowSyntheticDefaultImports": true,
        "strict": true,
        "forceConsistentCasingInFileNames": true,
        "module": "esnext",
        "moduleResolution": "node",
        "resolveJsonModule": true,
        "isolatedModules": false,
        "noEmit": false,
        "jsx": "react"
```

```
    },
    "include": ["**/*.ts", "../node_modules/cypress"]
}
```

6. Create a file called `webpack.config.js` under the `cypress` folder that contains the following code. This will help Cucumber pick up the step definition test cases with the `.ts` file extension and the executable specification files with the `.feature` file extension:

```
module.exports = {
  resolve: {
    extensions: [".tsx", ".ts", ".js"]
  },
  node: {
    fs: "empty",
    child_process: "empty",
    readline: "empty"
  },
  module: {
    rules: [{
        test: /\.spec.ts$/,
        exclude: [/node_modules/],
        use: [{
          loader: "ts-loader"
        }]
      },
      {
        test: /\.feature$/,
        use: [{
          loader: "cypress-cucumber-preprocessor/loader"
        }]
      }
    ]
  }
};
```

7. Create a file called `index.d.ts` under the `cypress/support/` directory of the app by using the following code. This will help TypeScript recognize the Cypress namespace and its chainable functions:

```
declare namespace Cypress {
  interface Chainable {
    /**
     * Custom command to select DOM element by data-cy
       attribute.
     * @example cy.dataCy('greeting')
     */
    dataCy(value: string): Chainable<Element>
  }
}
```

8. Delete all the `.js` and `.json` files under the `cypress/plugins`, `cypress/support`, `cypress/fixtures`, and `cypress/integration` folders since those are the examples for JavaScript projects.

9. Create a file called `index.ts` under the `cypress/plugins` folder that contains the following code for webpack integration, which is what we used for TypeScript integration:

```
const cucumber: any = require('cypress-cucumber-
preprocessor').default
const webpack: any = require('@cypress/webpack-
preprocessor')
// cypress/plugins/index.ts
/// <reference types="cypress" />


/**
 * @type {Cypress.PluginConfig}
 */
module.exports = (on: any, config: any) => {
  // `on` is used to hook into various events Cypress
emits
  // `config` is the resolved Cypress config
  on('file:preprocessor', cucumber())

  const options = {
```

```
    webpackOptions: require('../webpack.config.js')
  }

  on('file:preprocessor', webpack(options))
}
```

With that, we have set up Cypress, Cucumber, and Mocha for BDD and Living Documentation. In the next section, we will learn how to write a proper User Story with the executable specification in Gherkin.

Understanding the workflow to leverage BDD

To do BDD properly in any businesses, we should consider the following workflow. We will show you all the essential examples throughout this chapter:

1. Share a common understanding of the desired behavior of the solution or a feature between the business and technical teams via a conversation.

2. Capturing the conversation as a User Story with the Gherkin syntax, which the system uses to check against the desired system behavior automatically through test automation.

3. The development team needs to fulfill the desired system behavior by writing test cases (step definitions) and the actual code to build the system.

4. Deploy the increment (frontend and backend artifacts) to an environment that can be accessed by both the business and technical teams automatically through the DevOps pipeline.

5. Perform e2e test automation automatically.

6. Generate Living Documentation in any format, such as text or video, automatically that the Business team can access to provide feedback to the technical team.

7. The business team can choose the approval process between releasing new features to production in a batch manually or releasing new features automatically via the DevOps pipeline.

> **Tip**
>
> Cucumber is a very well-known and polished tool that has been used for many years for BDD. Since it is open source, the open source community has written open sourced Cucumber libraries for most modern programming languages, including TypeScript. This is why we have picked Cucumber in this chapter – because it can achieve the two main objectives:
>
> -Understanding the executable specification (Gherkin).
>
> -Running test cases (step definitions) against the executable specification, which checks the system's behavior.

Writing executable User Stories in Gherkin

Writing executable User Stories with Specification by Examples in Gherkin requires some practice. Gherkin is a domain-specific language for creating concrete examples of how a system should interact with the user in plain English, which everyone in the business can understand. The more you practice, the more you will get used to it quickly. So, let's start with a few common scenarios that will help you create a couple of feature files. Remember that each feature file can have multiple scenarios, just like each User Story can have multiple scenarios (also known as Specification by Example or Executable Specification). You can see this variation in the following examples:

- A simple feature that requires no user input:

```
Feature: A short description of the feature

   User story of the feature goes here

    Rule: Business rule goes here

    Description about the business rule

   Scenario: Description of a concrete example
     Given some context to set the scene
     And more context if needed
     When an action or interaction happens
     And more action if needed
     Then the outcome of the action should happen
     And more outcome if needed
```

- For a scenario that requires simple input, we use double quotation marks for the inputs. This means we can change the test value of the user input right from the scenario itself. It is very handy for mimicking real-world examples such as a person's name, age, item number, or even the total amount of their shopping cart. We shall consider writing this scenario with examples that are as concrete as possible. Let's create a pseudo-scenario with a concrete example of me buying a cheeseburger at Maccas:

```
Scenario: Adrian bought a cheese burger at Maccas
    Given "Adrian" the customer is very hungry
    And he has "50" bucks in his pocket
    When he ordered a "cheese burger" that cost "10"
    bucks
    And he paid "50" bucks at the counter
    Then he should get "40" bucks back
    And he should get a "cheese burger" at the counter
```

- If we have a scenario that requires multiple inputs to test the behavior of the system more thoroughly, then we should consider using a scenario outline with a data table. We should use square brackets, < >, plus double quotation marks, " ", for the input variables in the data table. Let's create another concrete example of me ordering multiple items from Maccas:

```
Scenario Outline: Adrian bought a meal at Maccas
    Given "Adrian" is super hungry
    And he has a "50" bucks gift card in his pocket
    When he orders the "<item>" that cost "<bucks>"
    And he paid with his gift card at the counter
    Then he should get "30" bucks back
    But not "20" bucks
    Then he should get his meal at the counter

    Examples: A customized cheese burger meal
      | item          | bucks |
      | cheese burger | 10    |
      | large coke    | 5     |
      | medium fries  | 5     |
```

This example demonstrated how to use the `Given`, `When`, `Then`, `And`, and `But` keywords, as well as the data table with multiple variables. In a real-world scenario, we might consider creating the user, called Adrian, in our backend database as a test user, and a gift card with 50 dollars credit on it associated with his account. When he purchases the items from the restaurant, the system will deduct the total amount of the meal from his gift card, and also adjust the inventory of each item in the shop. The developer should focus on writing test cases (also known as step definitions) to complete this scenario, which we will be discussing in the next section, and write the actual code of the application to fulfil the test scenario. Once the developer has committed the code to the repository, the DevOps pipeline will run through the build, test, and deploy stages, all the way to an environment that can be accessed by the team. This is what we called BDD.

Let's familiarize ourselves with the concept of BDD. Remember that in a real-world situation, there should always be a conversation between the business team, such as product owner and domain experts, and the technical team, such as the developers, designers, and testers, or even the users of the system regarding the context of the User Story to come up with several concrete examples. These examples should cover most or all of the possible scenarios. Let's create our very first example for the app we have been developing in the previous chapters.

Let's create a file called `Share_a_story.feature` in the `cypress/integration` folder. You can create as many subfolders as you want if you have an epic feature that has multiple User Stories. Enter the following text for the User Story to the feature file that we just created. This will also serve as a functional test by mimicking a real user scenario with a persona that shares a story on the app that we've built:

```
Feature: Share a story

    Adrian wants to share some stories,
    so that more people can know about his stories

    Rule: Share a story with at least the title and content

        This allows people would see the title on their feed
        and
        the content of the story itself

    Scenario: Adrian shares a story
        Given Adrian has a story to share
```

```
When he shares a story called "Hello" about "World"
Then people can see a story called "Hello" about
"World"
```

If you want to categorize functional and non-functional features, you can use the `Ability` keyword for functional features and `Business Needs` for non-functional features. In the next section, we will show you how to write step definitions to fulfil these features.

Writing test cases as step definitions with TypeScript

In this section, we will show you how to create step definitions to fulfil the feature file that we created in the previous section. A step definition is the actual implementation of the executable Specification by Examples. This means that we have the User Story in plain English so that both the business and technical teams will understand it. Then, we fulfil it with the code of the actual app and ensure that each step of the test case will pass each user scenario. The recommended procedure for BDD would be as follows:

1. Come up with a User Story with **Specification by Examples (SBE)** first.

2. The development team will pick up the executable specification and run it. The console will tell you that there is a failed test case that we need to implement for the step definitions.

3. Write some code for the actual app that can pass the test case.

4. Write the step definitions and rerun the tests.

5. Refactor the code of the app and step definitions until you pass the test case.

Let's create a file called `Share_a_story.spec.ts` in the `cypress/support/step_definitions/` directory, which you may also need to create by yourself. Then, follow these steps:

1. Import the step definition keywords from the `cypress-cucumber-preprocessor` for the actual test steps:

```
import { Given, When, Then } from 'cypress-cucumber-preprocessor/steps'
```

2. In a real-world scenario, you might want to make sure that Adrian has an account in the system. Then, you can log him in first so that he can access the page that can share his story. For our example, we just need to visit the page:

```
const url = 'http://localhost:3000'
Given('Adrian has a story to share', () => {
    cy.visit(url)
})
```

3. Share the actual story, along with its title and content, by entering the inputs and hitting the `create-button` in Cypress. As you can see, the title and content are input parameters that can be changed on the feature itself. This gives the team the flexibility to test different kinds of input values:

```
When('he shares a story called {string} about {string}',
(title, content) => {
    cy.get('input[placeholder="Title"]').type(title)
    cy.get('textarea[placeholder="Content"]').type(content)
    cy.get('.create-button').click()
})
```

4. Check the shared story with the matching title and the content of the other stories:

```
Then('people can see a story called {string} about
{string}', (title, content) => {
    cy.get('.post-title').contains(title)
    cy.get('.post-content').contains(content)
})
```

The preceding code shows us how to import the Cucumber step definition keywords that match the Gherkin syntax. We are telling Cypress to open the browser and visit the local host in our code to mimic the user, who would typically open a browser and visit the website, just like we did when we run the website locally. Then, we can tell Cypress to enter the title and the content of the story, as well as to click the `create-button` to create the story. As you can see, Gherkin is very flexible in terms of how you change the test data through the scenarios instead of modifying the code. This is very useful when the business team or the technical team wants to change the test data to test the system's behavior, without changing the step definition code – only the feature file itself has to be changed.

Let's run the yarn start command in the Terminal first to start the app and then open a second Terminal and run the yarn e2e command. The result of the test will be printed in the Terminal:

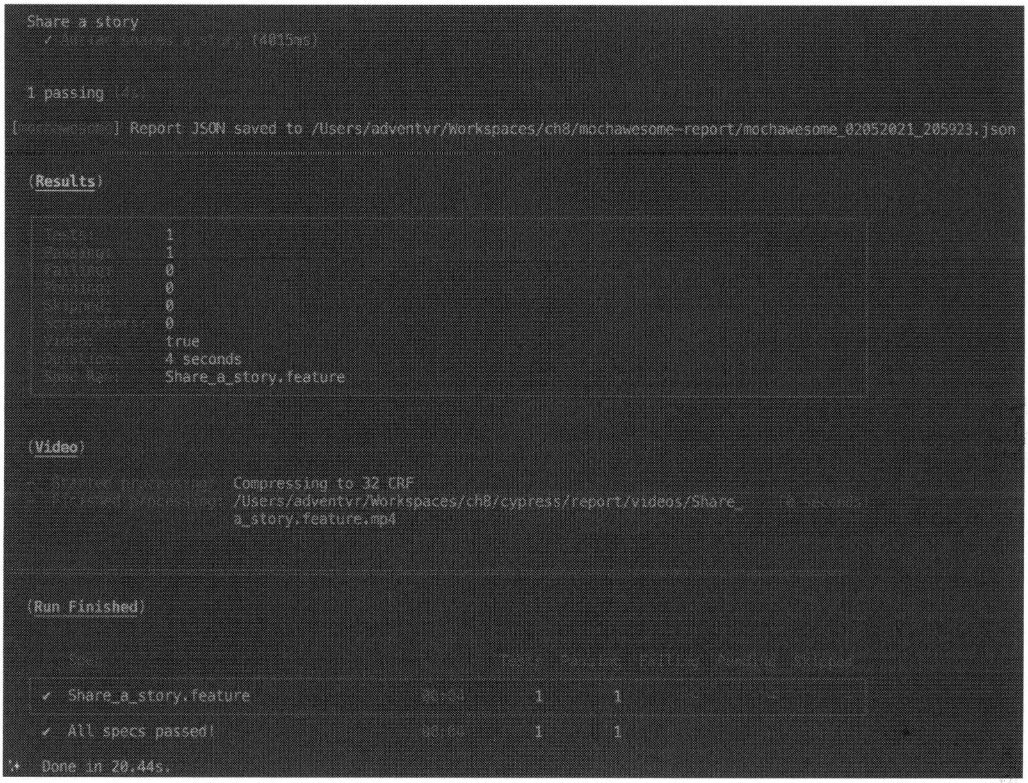

```
Share a story
  ✓ Adrian shares a story (4015ms)

1 passing (4s)
[mochawesome] Report JSON saved to /Users/adventvr/Workspaces/ch8/mochawesome-report/mochawesome_02052021_205923.json

(Results)

  Tests:        1
  Passing:      1
  Failing:      0
  Pending:      0
  Skipped:      0
  Screenshots:  0
  Video:        true
  Duration:     4 seconds
  Spec Ran:     Share_a_story.feature

(Video)

  Started processing:  Compressing to 32 CRF
  Finished processing: /Users/adventvr/Workspaces/ch8/cypress/report/videos/Share_    8 seconds
                       a_story.feature.mp4

(Run Finished)

        Spec                          Tests  Passing  Failing  Pending  Skipped
  ✓  Share_a_story.feature           00:04      1        1
  ✓  All specs passed!               00:04      1        1
✨  Done in 20.44s.
```

Figure 8.2 – Cucumber test result in the Terminal

The test results show you how many of the tests failed and passed, as well as how many seconds it took per test and their total duration. These results can also produce video captures of all the tests and test reports in HTML or JSON format. We chose JSON format here because the build pipeline can pick up the JSON report and show it on the Amplify Console.

If you followed the path of the captured video, you should be able to see that Cypress opened a browser, visited the landing page, and checked that the HTML page's title is `React App`, as follows:

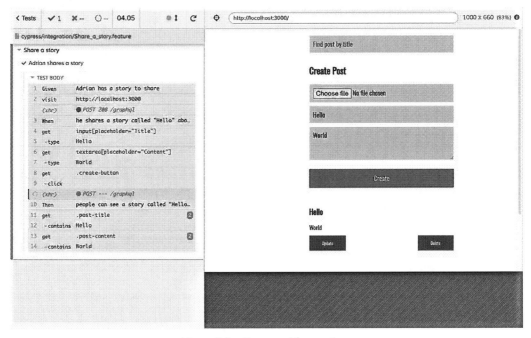

Figure 8.3 – Cypress video capture

Imagine that there are hundreds of test cases that must go through a sophisticated end-to-end regression test repeatedly, whenever you want to deploy new features to production. It would take an enormous amount of time and manpower to achieve such a big task. But thanks to technology, we can simply run all these end-to-end tests locally or commit the code and let the DevOps pipeline run them on the cloud. You will be provided with the results when the run is completed.

> **Tip**
> For more information about Cypress, you can check out the Cypress documentation (`https://docs.cypress.io/api/`).

Now, let's learn how to integrate Cypress with the DevOps pipeline.

Integrating Cypress with the DevOps pipeline

In this section, we will show you how to add the e2e test phase to the DevOps pipeline. At the time of writing, Cypress only works on the root directory with a single app. If you have a monorepo that contains many apps, then you will need to create a new repository and create an Amplify app to enable the e2e test.

If you set your Amplify app to manual deployment earlier in this book, then you might want to change Amplify Hosting to continuous deployment instead of manual deployment. You can run the `amplify add hosting` command again to select continuous deployment. This will take care of integrating the DevOps pipeline with the Amplify app:

```
amplify add hosting
? Select the plugin module to execute Hosting with Amplify
Console (Managed hosting with custom domains, Continuous
deployment)
? Choose a type Continuous deployment (Git-based deployments)
? Continuous deployment is configured in the Amplify Console.
Please hit enter once you connect your repository
Amplify hosting urls:
| FrontEnd Env | Domain                                     |
| master       | https://master.xxxxxxxxx.amplifyapp.com |
```

The AWS Amplify Console allows you to edit the build settings directly. Alternatively, you can choose to edit the `amplify.yml` file in the repository – either should work fine. The build settings on the Amplify Console will override the ones in the GitHub repository, so if the default settings of the `amplify.yml` file's build settings are not the same as the ones in the repository, you might want to visit the Amplify Console page to change them. Follow these steps to enable the test phase with the build pipeline:

1. Let's open the `amplify.yml` file and enter the following code:

```
version: 2
backend:
  phases:
    preBuild:
      commands:
        - nvm use $VERSION_NODE_12
        - "# Execute Amplify CLI with the helper script"
        - amplifyPush --simple
```

```
      build:
        commands:
          - nvm use $VERSION_NODE_12
          - yarn install
frontend:
  phases:
    preBuild:
      commands:
        - nvm use $VERSION_NODE_12
        - yarn install
    build:
      commands:
        - nvm use $VERSION_NODE_12
        - yarn build
  artifacts:
    baseDirectory: build
    files:
      - "**/*"
  cache:
    paths:
      - node_modules/**/*
```

2. We will add the test steps to the YML file. These tell the pipeline to start the app at localhost on port 3000 and then run the end-to-end test. Generate the Living Documentation at the end, which is the recorded video in our case:

```
test:
  artifacts:
    baseDirectory: cypress
    configFilePath: "**/mochawesome.json"
    files:
      - "**/*.png"
      - "**/*.mp4"
  phases:
    preTest:
      commands:
        - nvm use $VERSION_NODE_12
        - yarn add wait-on pm2
        - npx pm2 start npm -- start
        - "npx wait-on http://localhost:3000"
    test:
      commands:
        - nvm use $VERSION_NODE_12
        - yarn e2e
    postTest:
      commands:
        - nvm use $VERSION_NODE_12
        - yarn doc & yarn report
```

3. Now, open the Amplify Console page in the browser, go to **Build settings**, and click the **Edit** button:

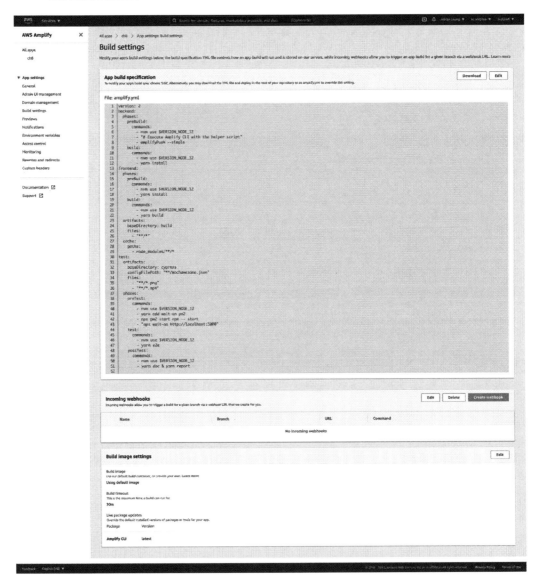

Figure 8.4 – Editing the build settings through the Amplify Console

4. Copy and paste the code from *step 1* into the text area and click the **Save** button:

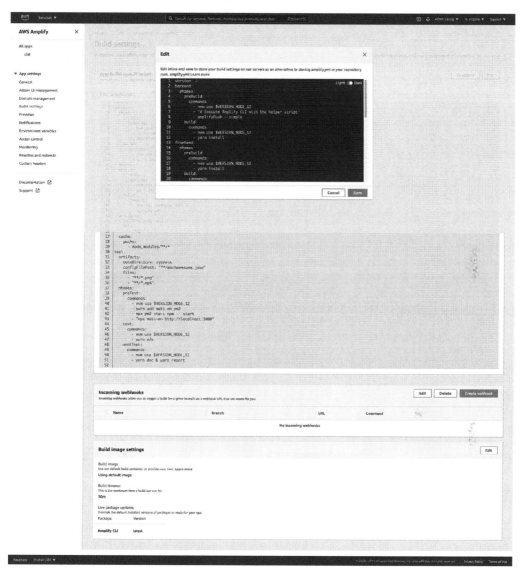

Figure 8.5 – Saving the build settings

5. Now, commit the changes to the repository, especially the `amplify.yml` file. We should see that the DevOps pipeline has been triggered automatically:

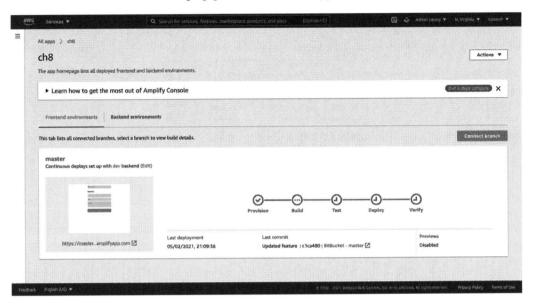

Figure 8.6 – The DevOps pipeline with the test step being trigged automatically

6. It might take around 10 minutes the first time you do this, but the subsequent build time should be much faster. This example should take around 7 minutes to complete because the node modules have been cached. You can click on the **Test** section to check out what has been tested:

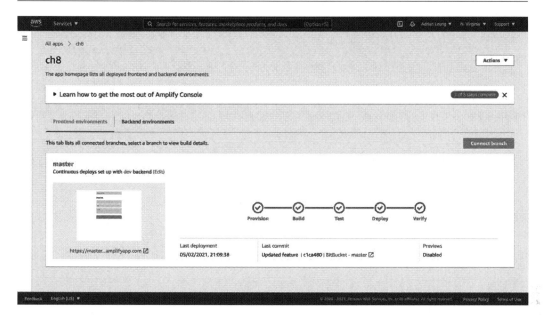

Figure 8.7 – The DevOps pipeline with the test step being trigged automatically

7.   As you can see, the test has passed. We can click on the **View log** button to check out the console log of the test:

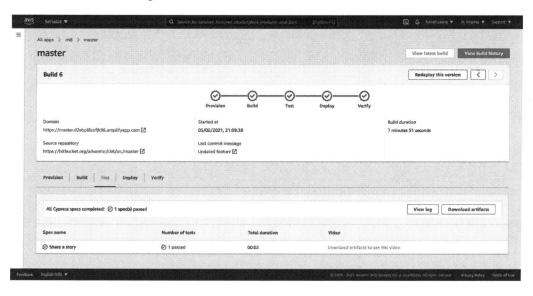

Figure 8.8 – The DevOps pipeline with the test step being trigged automatically

8. The log should be similar to the log in the Terminal when we ran the end-to-end test locally on our machine. We can click on the **Download artifacts** button to download the captured test video, which should be the same as the one that was generated locally, too:

Figure 8.9 – The DevOps pipeline with the test step being trigged automatically

9. If we click on the **Domain** URL on the dashboard, it should lead us to the deployed environment:

Figure 8.10 – Checking out the deployed Amplify app

This must be a lot to take in as this has given you an overall idea of how BDD and end-to-end test automation work. Don't stop here, though – try to create an app and create more User Stories to test different scenarios based on different use cases. The more you practice BDD with Cucumber, the more you will realize that is a great way to shorten the overall development cycle.

Summary

In this chapter, we learned how to use Cypress and Cucumber to achieve BDD and test automation in one go. BDD and end-to-end test automation help in bridging the communication gap between the business team and the technical team, as it allows them to communicate directly to come up with SBE that have a common understanding. This will greatly reduce the rework rate of the upcoming project for your company.

The AWS Amplify pipeline takes this to the next level by handling all the Ops for the development team. All you need to do is configure the actual DevOps steps; the pipeline will be taking care of itself. I would call it NoOps since most of the Ops have been handled by the Amplify pipeline. Now, you only need to focus on shipping new features to the customer instead of fiddling around with the DevOps pipeline and test automation toolchains.

In the next chapter, we will show you how to set up a custom domain for your web app and the latest add-on to the AWS Amplify ecosystem in 2021, called the Admin UI.

9
Setting Up a Custom Domain Name and the Amplify Admin UI

Welcome to *Chapter 9*, *Setting Up a Custom Domain Name and the Amplify Admin UI* – we've made it! It is time to publish your app on a website and then tell the world about it. In this chapter, we will show you how to purchase a domain name through AWS Route 53 and then hook that up to your Amplify app. AWS Amplify can connect to the domain name that you purchase through the AWS Route 53 service seamlessly. We will also show you how to connect the Amplify app with third-party DNS services such as GoDaddy. After that, we will show you how to set up the Admin UI in order to manage the content of the app. By doing this, you will be able to invite others to help you edit the content on your website. The Admin UI is like a traditional CMS that you can create, edit, and delete the content of a website or an app with. It is especially useful when you have dedicated team members to either create or moderate the content of your app.

In this chapter, we will cover the following topics:

- Adding a custom domain name in AWS Route 53
- Adding a custom domain name using a third-party DNS provider
- Setting up the Amplify Admin UI (beta)
- Walking through the Amplify Admin UI

If you have followed along with this book, you should have an Amplify app that is written in React or React Native. As we mentioned previously, both React Native and Expo apps can be exported as web apps. Therefore, you can publish your app online with a dedicated domain name, as well as mobile app stores.

Technical requirements

To complete this chapter, you will need to have completed the exercises of all the previous chapters. This will help you understand the benefits of setting up a domain name and enabling the Admin UI.

Adding a custom domain name to AWS Route 53

So far, we have built a simple app that can let people create posts with text and images. Now, it is time to tell the world about our accomplishments. The best way to do that is to set up an easy-to-remember domain name that shows the meaning of your product itself. AWS offers a wide range of products that can help you take your business and product from zero to one. This includes Route 53, which lets you buy a domain name directly through AWS, without shopping for your domain name on a different platform. The good thing about choosing a single platform that provides the entire ecosystem of your digital product is that you can keep all your bills in a single invoice, instead of on multiple invoices. Let's go to the AWS Amplify Console:

1. First, go to the Route 53 dashboard (`https://console.aws.amazon.com/route53`). Then, enter the domain name that you want to purchase and hit the **Check** button to see if the domain is still up for purchase:

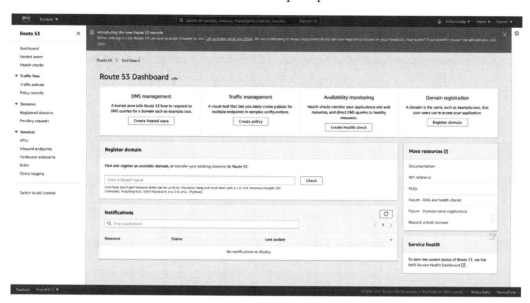

Figure 9.1 – Route 53 – Finding and registering for an available domain name

You can find a domain name by looking for domain name extensions such as `.com`, `.net`, and so on. If you cannot find the domain name extension that you want, then you might want to purchase a domain name from a third-party DNS provider, which will be covered in the next section.

2. You will see if your domain name is available, along with various domain extensions. You can add more than one domain name to the cart to purchase multiple domain names at once. Once you've found what you want, you can simply click the **Continue** button:

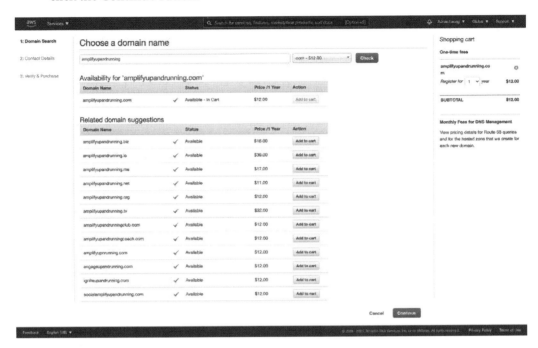

Figure 9.2 – Route 53 – Choosing a domain name

You can purchase multiple domain names at once, as well as select the number of years you wish to register for, from here.

3. Enter the registrant contact details of your domain name. Normally, this is the address of your company and the contact details of the administrator. You can always enable the privacy protection feature to hide some contact details, such as your email address and the physical address from WHOIS.com. Only law enforcement can request the actual contact details if something happens to the domain name. Alternatively, you can enter your PO Box details for the address if you want someone to contact you but without knowing your actual address. Once you've done this, click the **Continue** button:

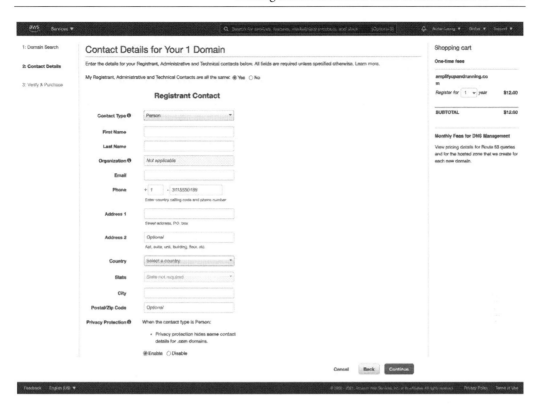

Figure 9.3 – Route53 – Registrant contact details

You can always leave privacy protection off if you want people to be able to find you through the WHOIS database via your business's contact details.

4. Now, visit the Amplify Console of the app and go to the **Domain management** section from the left-hand side menu. Click on the **Add domain** button at the top-right corner of the page:

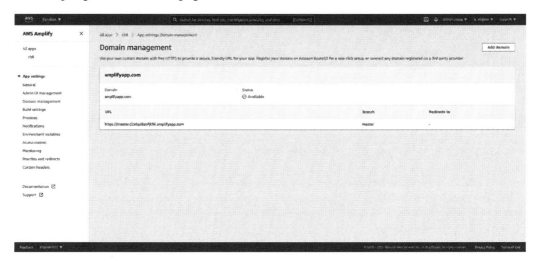

Figure 9.4 – Amplify Console – Domain management section

5. Enter the domain name that you just purchased from Route 53 and click the **Configure domain** button:

Figure 9.5 – Amplify Console – Finding a domain

This feature works with a domain name that has been purchased through AWS Route 53 or external websites such as GoDaddy.

6. By default, your domain name from Route 53 will be configured as the root domain with `https://yourdomainname.com` and `https://www.yourdomainname.com`. You can remove or add a subdomain here directly. Each root domain and subdomain can be configured with a different branch of the repository of your app. You can also set up redirects to the Admin UI, which will be discussed in the *Walking through the Amplify Admin UI* section of this chapter. Once you are done, click the **Save** button:

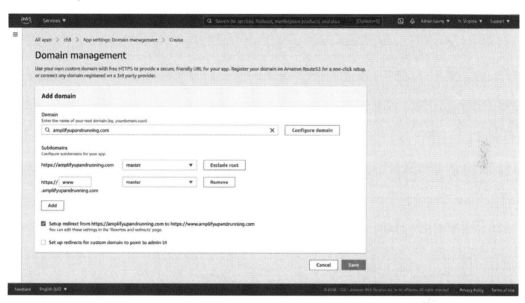

Figure 9.6 – Amplify Console – Subdomain setup

All SSL certificate, root domain, and subdomain names can be configured directly from here, as long as they're directly related to the Amplify app. This includes the branch of the repository and the Admin UI's URL.

7. Once you've done this, the **Secure Sockets Layer** (**SSL**) certificate will be created and the **Domain Name System** (**DNS**) will be propagated within 24 hours. Then, your app will be available on the new domain name. Its format will be `https://yourdomainname.com`.

All you need to do now is periodically check the status of the DNS verification, SSL creation, and DNS propagation processes. Once you've done this, you can access your AWS Amplify app directly from the registered domain name.

Adding a custom domain name using a third-party DNS provider

Many of us might have purchased some domain names through various DNS providers. This section will give you an idea of how to easily hook up your existing domain name to the Amplify app. The only difference between setting up a domain name through Route 53 and a third-party DNS provider is the verification steps. If you have already owned or purchased a domain name through a third-party DNS provider, follow these steps to configure it with the AWS Amplify Console:

1. Go to the **Domain management** dashboard via the AWS Amplify Console and enter the domain name that you have just purchased from the third-party DNS provider (GoDaddy, in our case). Then, click the **Configure domain** button:

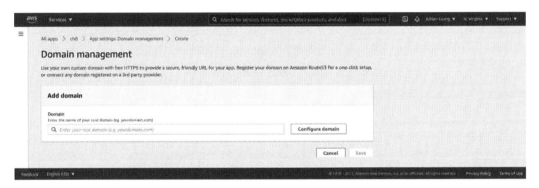

Figure 9.7 – Amplify Console – Finding a domain

This feature works with a domain name that has been purchased through AWS Route 53 or external websites such as GoDaddy.

2. By default, the domain name you've purchased from a third-party domain name provider will be configured as the root domain with `https://yourdomainname.com` and `https://www.yourdomainname.com`. You can add or remove the subdomain here directly. Each root domain and subdomain can be configured with a different branch of the repository of your app. You can also set up redirects to the Admin UI too, which will be discussed in the *Walking through the Amplify Admin UI* section of this chapter. Once you are done, click **Save** and wait up to 24 hours for the **DNS** to be propagated and the free **SSL** to be generated for your domain name:

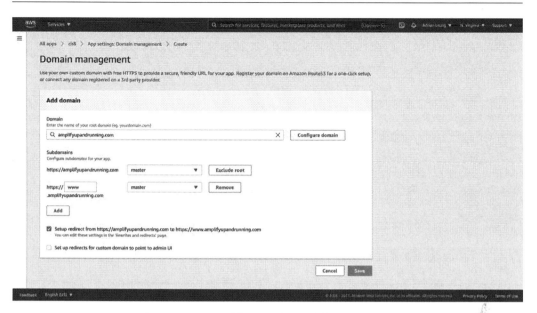

Figure 9.8 – Amplify Console – Subdomains setup

All SSL certificate, root domain, and subdomain names can be configured directly from here, as long as they're directly related to the Amplify app. This includes the branch of the repository and the Admin UI's URL.

3. The SSL creation process requires a verification step to be completed; that is, copying the CNAME key-value pair that was generated through the **Domain management** console, as follows:

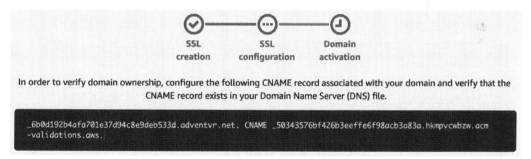

Figure 9.9 – Amplify Console – DNS verification

4. Go to the third-party domain name DNS provider's DNS management dashboard (`https://dcc.godaddy.com/manage/dns`) (GoDaddy, in our case) and enter the domain name that you own:

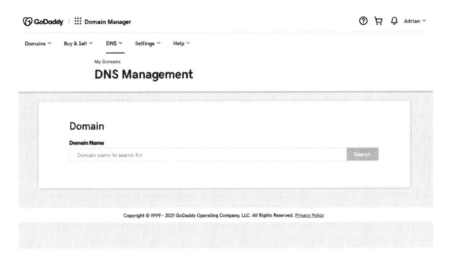

Figure 9.10 – GoDaddy – DNS management

5. Click the **Add** button of the **Records** section to add DNS settings:

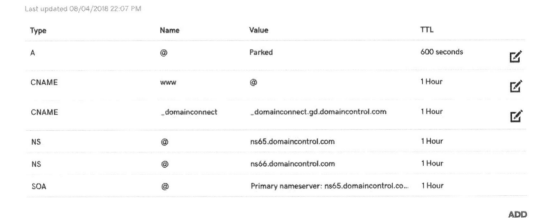

Figure 9.11 – GoDaddy – DNS records

6. Select **CNAME** via the **Type** dropdown selector:

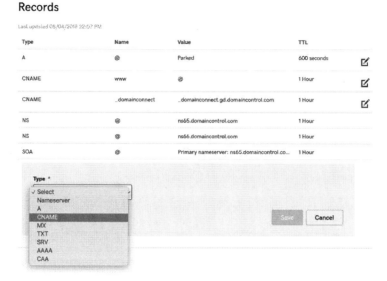

Figure 9.12 – GoDaddy – Adding a DNS CNAME record

7. Enter the **CNAME** key-value pair into the **Host** (key) and **Point to** (value) text fields and click the **Save** button:

Records

Last updated 08/04/2018 22:07 PM

Type	Name	Value	TTL	
A	@	Parked	600 seconds	✎
CNAME	www	@	1 Hour	✎
CNAME	_domainconnect	_domainconnect.gd.domaincontrol.com	1 Hour	✎
NS	@	ns65.domaincontrol.com	1 Hour	
NS	@	ns66.domaincontrol.com	1 Hour	
SOA	@	Primary nameserver: ns65.domaincontrol.co...	1 Hour	

Type *	Host *	Points to *
CNAME		

TTL *
1 Hour

Save   Cancel

Figure 9.13 – GoDaddy – Entering a CNAME DNS record

8. Once you've done this, go back to the **Domain management** section of the Amplify app via the AWS Amplify Console. Click on the **Actions** dropdown menu and click on the **View DNS records** button to find the DNS record's settings:

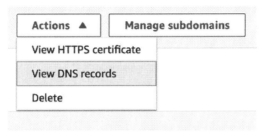

Figure 9.13 – Amplify Console – View DNS records option

9. Copy both DNS records and create the same records through the third-party DNS provider, as we did in *steps 12* to *14*. We will need to create two records this time called **ANAME** and **CNAME**, as follows:

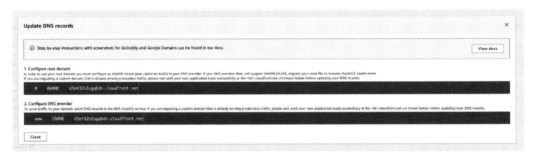

Figure 9.14 – Amplify Console – Copying the DNS ANAME and CNAME records

10. Once you've done this, the SSL certificate will be created and the DNS will be propagated within 24 hours. Then, your app will be available on the new domain name. Its format will be `https://yourdomainname.com`.

All you need to do now is periodically check the status of the DNS verification, SSL creation, and DNS propagation properly. Once you've done this, you can access your AWS Amplify app directly from the registered domain name.

In this section, we learned how to set up a custom domain name for our web app or website. In the next section, we will show you how to set up the Amplify Admin UI as the **content management system (CMS)** for your web and mobile apps.

Setting up the Amplify Admin UI (beta)

The Admin UI is still in beta (in early 2021), which means some of the features are still in preview version. The Admin UI is like a traditional CMS where you can maintain the content of your website. You can create a data model directly from the Admin UI, but it might crash the app if the model between the app in production and the admin are different. So, it is safer to update and create a data model when you are building the app. Try not to update the data model with the app that is in production. Apart from that, you can grant access to your system admins, content creators, content moderators, and so on so that they can maintain the content of your Amplify app. This saves you hundreds of hours building the CMS system from scratch. Let's set up the Admin UI:

1. Go to the Amplify Console of your Amplify app, select **Admin UI management** from the left-hand side menu, and click on the toggle for **Enable admin UI (All environments)** to switch it from off to on:

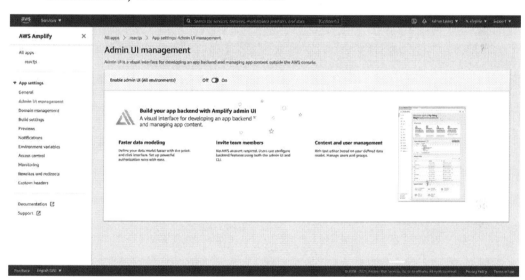

Figure 9.15 – Amplify Console – Amplify Admin UI entry point

2. Invite users to the Admin UI by clicking the **Invite users** button in the **Access control settings** section:

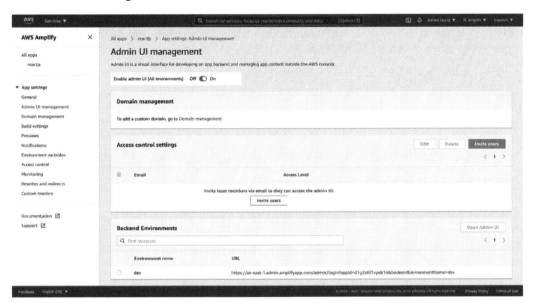

Figure 9.16 – Amplify Console – Enabling the Amplify Admin UI

3. You can invite multiple users to access the Amplify Admin UI with different access levels. I would recommend granting **Full access** to admins only and granting **Manage only** access to the rest. This is because you don't want non-admins to be able to mess with either the data model or the user data. It is safer that way, just in case somebody has updated the data model accidentally and the end users might not be able to use the app in production. Once you've entered the email address and selected the access level, hit the **Send invite** button to send out the invitation:

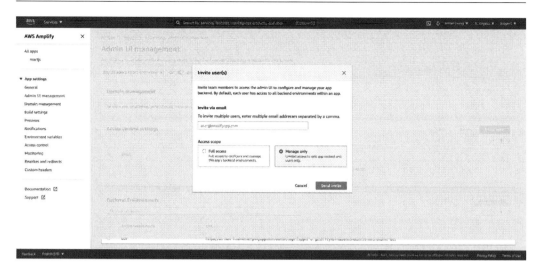

Figure 9.17 – Amplify Console – Inviting users to the Amplify Admin UI

4. The Admin UI URL is sitting at the bottom of the **Admin UI management** page of the Amplify App. Select the environment for the Admin UI, such as dev or production, and then click on the URL directly or click **Open Admin UI** on the right-hand side:

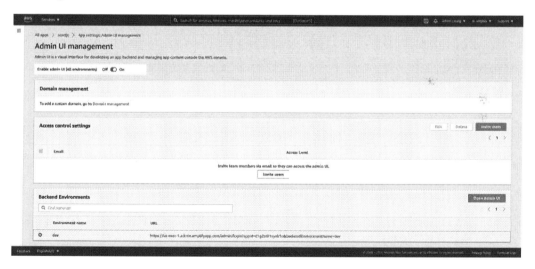

Figure 9.18 – Amplify Console – Amplify Admin UI URL

5. After a short initialization process, you will see a welcome message, as shown in *Figure 9.18*. Because it's still in beta, your data model may not appear on the **Data model** section of the Admin UI yet. If that is the case, click on the **View data model** button to find out:

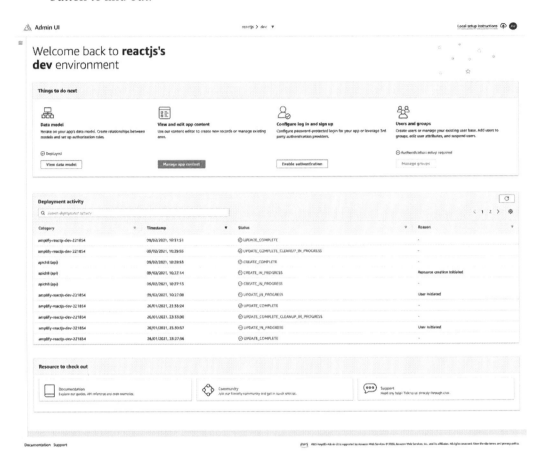

Figure 9.20 – Amplify Admin UI dashboard

6. If you cannot see the data model of your Amplify App here, simply click on the **Enable DataStore and deploy** button:

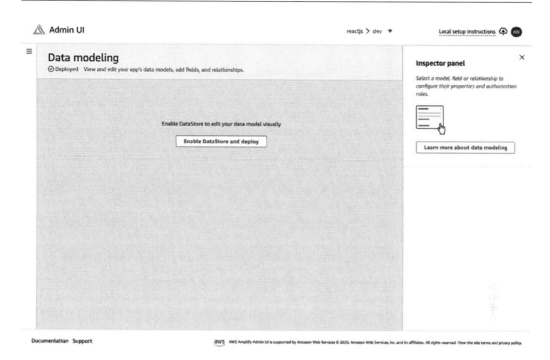

Figure 9.21 – Admin UI – Data modeling

7.   Enable the **DataStore** feature by clicking the **Deploy** button:

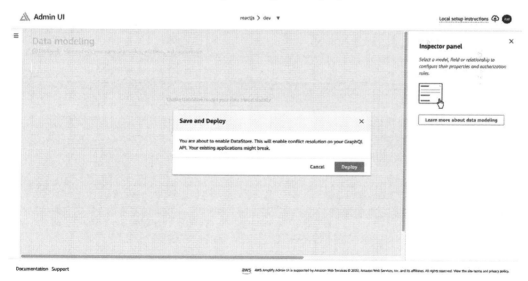

Figure 9.22 – Admin UI – Saving and deploying the data model

8.   Wait a few minutes for the data model to be deployed. You can click on the **Deploying…** link button in the top-right corner of the page to check the deployment's status:

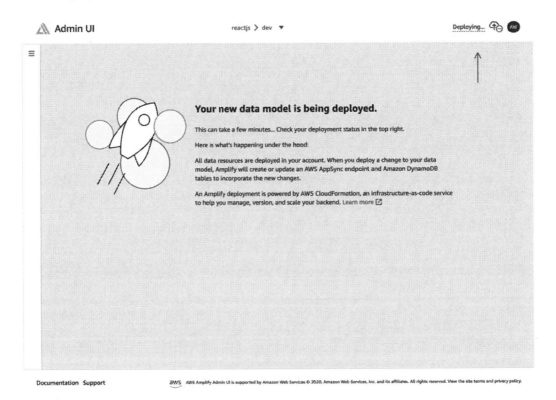

Figure 9.23 – Admin UI – Data model creation

9. Once the deployment process is complete, you will see that the data model looks exactly the same as the one we created in the previous chapters. It is safe to edit and add data models in the dev environment directly from here and create a relationship between the data models. Click the **Save and deploy** button once you've finished editing the data model:

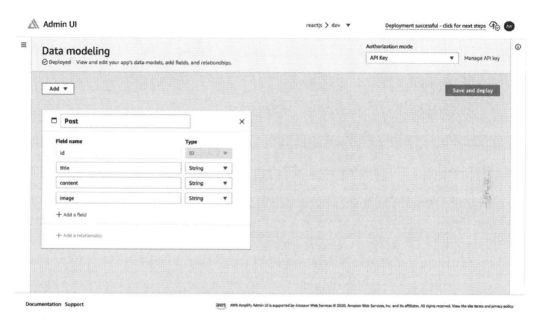

Figure 9.24 – Admin UI – Data modeling UI

10. Click on the **Create post** button to create new posts directly from the **Content** dashboard:

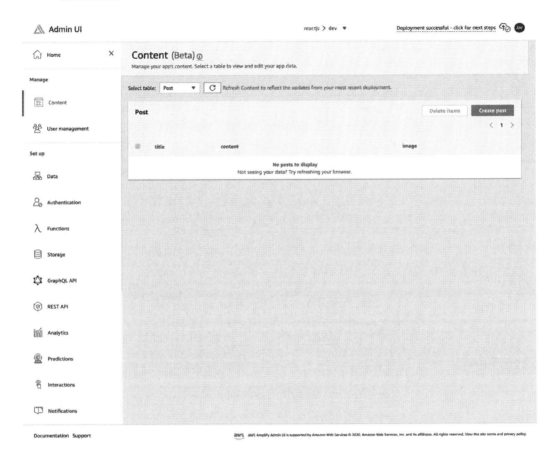

Figure 9.25 – Admin UI – Content dashboard

11. Enter the title and content of the post. You can click on the **Edit in markdown** link button of the text field to enable the rich text editor:

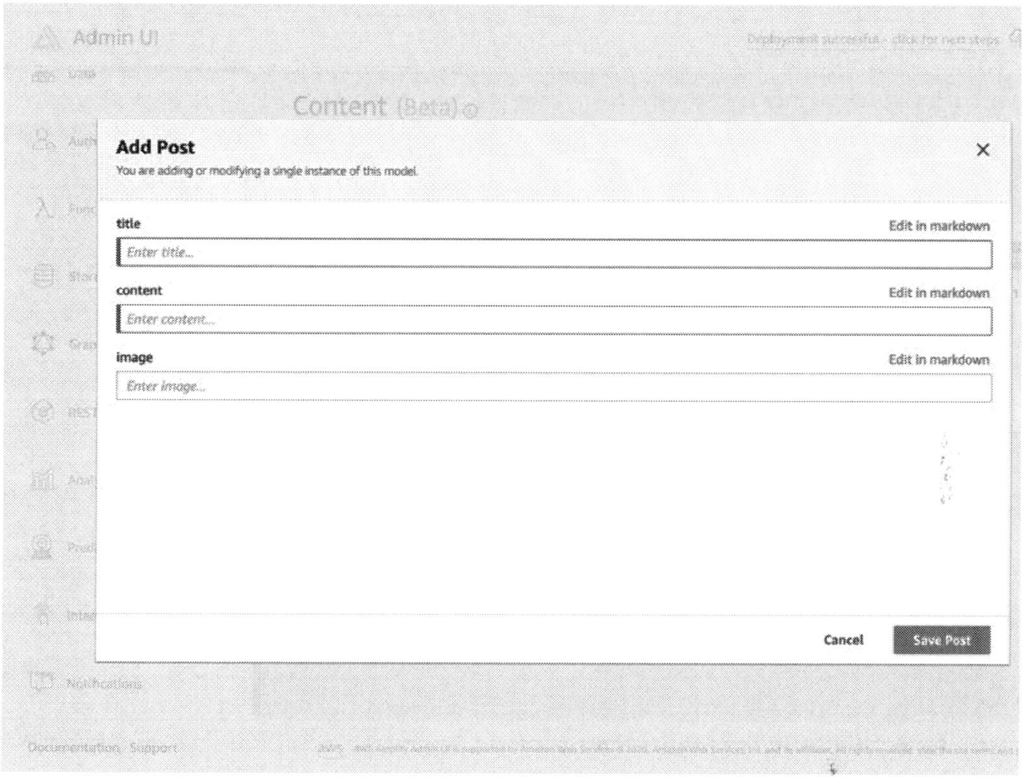

Figure 9.26 – Admin UI – Content dashboard – Add Post

12. You can use the rich text editor to create the content or the title of the app. This includes adding emojis, HTML code, style to the text, and so on directly from here. Click the **Save Post** button when you are done:

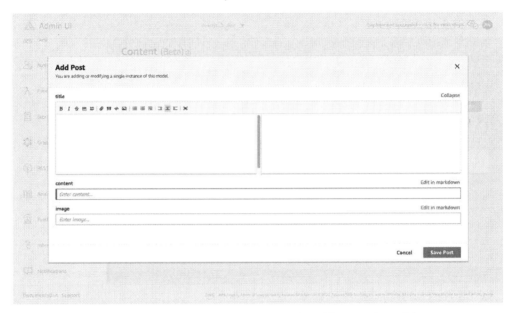

Figure 9.27 – Admin UI - Content dashboard – Add Post with markdown

13. As you can see, the new post has been added to the list. You can always click on the post itself directly to edit its content:

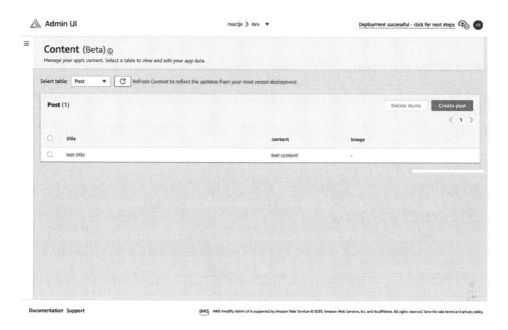

Figure 9.28 – Admin UI – Content – Posts

At this point, we should have a brief understanding of what the Admin UI can do with our Amplify app. We understand that we can do data modeling directly from the Admin UI, as long as we have **Full access** to that. Admins with **Manage only** access can help moderate this content through the Admin UI directly by going through the blog posts. In the next section, we will show you what additional features you can access directly from the Admin UI.

Walking through the Amplify Admin UI

In the previous section, we enabled the Admin UI and data modeling. In this section, we will go through a few Admin UI features that are related to our Amplify app:

1. Click on the **User management** button from the left-hand side menu. You will see the User Management console, which is a simplified version of the **Cognito** service that we mentioned earlier in this book. You can manage users and groups directly from here by clicking the **Set up authentication** button:

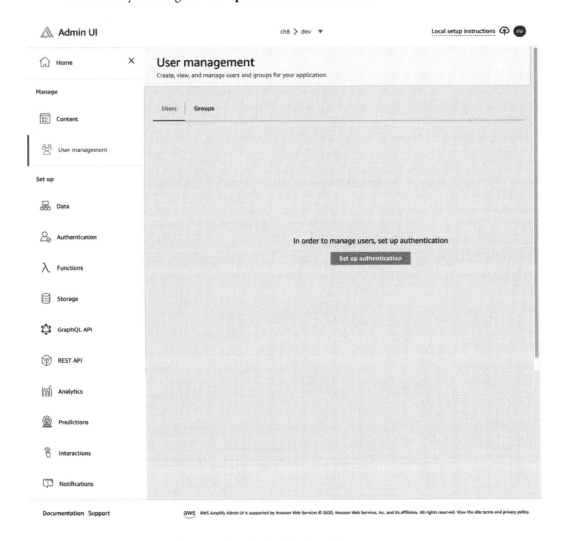

Figure 9.29 – Admin UI – User Management

2. Click on the **Authentication** button on the left-hand side menu. At this point, you
    will see the Authentication console, which is similar to the **Cognito** service that
    we mentioned earlier in this book. You can configure the login mechanism directly
    from here, such as email or phone only, or even **multi-factor authentication
    (MFA)**:

Figure 9.30 – Admin UI – Authentication

3. Click on the **Functions** button on the left-hand side menu. At this point, you will see instructions for how to add Lambda functions to your Amplify app. This is useful when your Amplify app requires features other than the basic **create, read, update and delete (CRUD)** operations of DynamoDB. For more information, you can click on the **Read more** button:

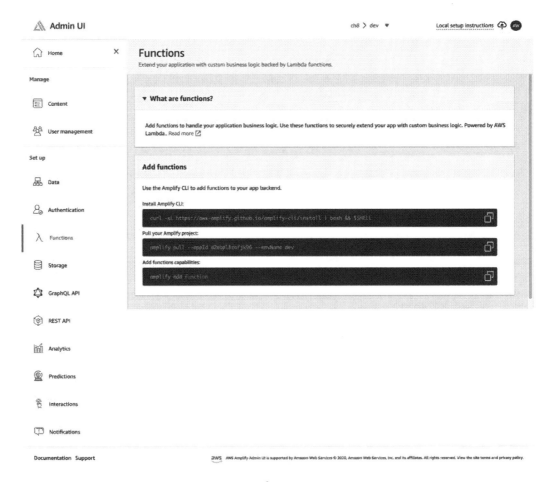

Figure 9.31 – Admin UI – Functions

4. Click on the **Storage** button on the left-hand side menu. Here, you will see instructions for how to add Amplify Storage to your Amplify app. We mentioned how to add Amplify Storage through the Amplify Console and S3 in the previous chapters. For more information, click on the **Read more** button:

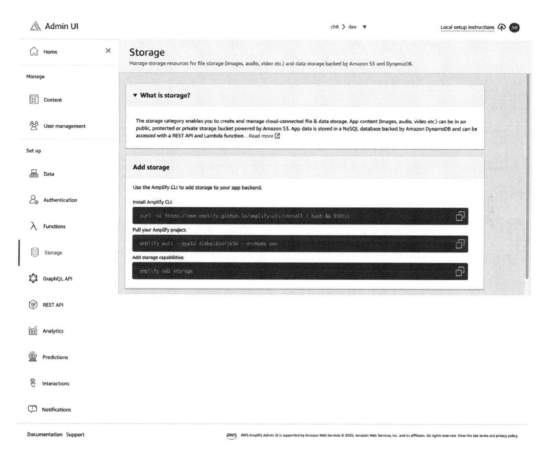

Figure 9.32 – Admin UI – Storage

5. Click on the **GraphQL** button on the left-hand side menu. Here, you will see instructions for how to add the GraphQL backend to your Amplify app. We mentioned how to add GraphQL through the Amplify Console and S3 in the previous chapters. For more information, can click on the **Read more** button. If you click on one of the deployed GraphQL resources, let's say **ch8** in our case, you will be taken to the **AWS AppSync** dashboard:

Figure 9.33 – Admin UI – GraphQL API

As you can see, the Admin UI is quite powerful in terms of managing the content and resources of the Amplify app. You can empower your team and peers to have different levels of access so that they can manage the Amplify app for you, such as support admins, who can help users with login issues, and content admins, who can edit and moderate blog posts.

Summary

In this chapter, you learned how to set up domain names and subdomain names for your Amplify app through AWS Route 53 and third-party DNS providers. At this point, you may have realized that building a cloud-native app from scratch and making it production-ready is quite easy with AWS Amplify. We even covered the latest Admin UI as an add-on feature for our app. When your user base grows a certain amount, you can no longer handle all the support requests from users. You have to find more admins to maintain the content and users of the app for you. With AWS Amplify and the Amplify UI, you save hundreds of hours creating CMSes and user management systems for your app.

I hope you enjoy your AWS Amplify journey from here on out! You can try out other additional features from the Admin UI, such as prediction, chatbot, analytics, and more by following the appropriate instructions and adding them to your Amplify app.

`Packt.com`

Subscribe to our online digital library for full access to over 7,000 books and videos, as well as industry leading tools to help you plan your personal development and advance your career. For more information, please visit our website.

Why subscribe?

- Spend less time learning and more time coding with practical eBooks and Videos from over 4,000 industry professionals

- Improve your learning with Skill Plans built especially for you

- Get a free eBook or video every month

- Fully searchable for easy access to vital information

- Copy and paste, print, and bookmark content

Did you know that Packt offers eBook versions of every book published, with PDF and ePub files available? You can upgrade to the eBook version at `packt.com` and as a print book customer, you are entitled to a discount on the eBook copy. Get in touch with us at `customercare@packtpub.com` for more details.

At `www.packt.com`, you can also read a collection of free technical articles, sign up for a range of free newsletters, and receive exclusive discounts and offers on Packt books and eBooks.

Other Books You May Enjoy

If you enjoyed this book, you may be interested in these other books by Packt:

Building Low-Code Applications with Mendix

Bryan Kenneweg , Imran Kasam , Micah McMullen

ISBN: 978-1-80020-142-2

- Gain a clear understanding of what low-code development is and the factors driving its adoption
- Become familiar with the various features of Mendix for rapid application development
- Discover concrete use cases of Studio Pro
- Build a fully functioning web application that meets your business requirements

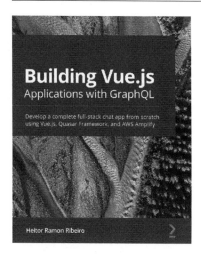

Building Vue.js Applications with GraphQL

Heitor Ramon Ribeiro

ISBN: 978-1-80056-507-4

- Set up your Vue.js projects with Vue CLI and explore the power of Vue components
- Discover steps to create functional components in Vue.js for faster rendering
- Become familiar with AWS Amplify and learn how to set up your environment
- Understand how to create your first GraphQL schema
- Use Quasar Framework to create simple and effective interfaces
- Discover effective techniques to create queries for interacting with data
- Explore Vuex for adding state management capabilities to your app

Packt is searching for authors like you

If you're interested in becoming an author for Packt, please visit authors.
packtpub.com and apply today. We have worked with thousands of developers and
tech professionals, just like you, to help them share their insight with the global tech
community. You can make a general application, apply for a specific hot topic that we are
recruiting an author for, or submit your own idea.

Share Your Thoughts

Now you've finished *Rapid Application Development with AWS Amplify,* we'd love to hear your thoughts! Scan the QR code below to go straight to the Amazon review page for this book and share your feedback or leave a review on the site that you purchased it from.

https://packt.link/r/1800207239

Your review is important to us and the tech community and will help us make sure we're delivering excellent quality content.

Index

Made in the USA
Coppell, TX
07 September 2021